Respect and Responsibility – Taking a Stand Against Anti-Social Behaviour

Presented to Parliament
by the Secretary of State for the Home Department
by Command of Her Majesty
March 2003

Cm 5778

£13.25

Ministerial Foreword

by the Home Secretary,
The Rt Hon David Blunkett MP

As a society, our rights as individuals are based on the sense of responsibility we have towards others and to our families and communities. This means respecting each other's property, respecting the streets and public places we share and respecting our neighbours' right to live free from harassment and distress. It is the foundation of a civic society.

This White Paper is all about this sense of responsibility: an acceptance that anti-social behaviour, in whatever guise, is not acceptable and that together we will take responsibility to stamp it out, whenever we come across it. This responsibility starts in the family, where parents are accountable for the actions of their children and set the standards they are to live by. It extends to neighbours, who should not have to endure noise nuisance. It continues into local communities, where people take pride in the appearance of estates and do not tolerate vandalism, litter or yobbish behaviour.

Our aim is a 'something for something' society where we treat one another with respect and where we all share responsibility for taking a stand against what is unacceptable.

But some people and some families undermine this. The anti-social behaviour of a few, damages the lives of many. We should never underestimate its impact. We have seen the way communities spiral downwards once windows get broken and are not fixed, graffiti spreads and stays there, cars are left abandoned, streets get grimier and dirtier, youths hang around street corners intimidating the elderly. The result: crime increases, fear goes up and people feel trapped.

It's time to stop thinking of anti-social behaviour as something that we can just ignore. Anti-social behaviour blights people's lives, destroys families and ruins communities. It holds back the regeneration of our disadvantaged areas and creates the environment in which crime can take hold.

That is why this document – building on existing measures such as Anti-Social Behaviour Orders that we have introduced over the last six years – sets out the Government's next steps for dealing urgently with this problem.

The practical solutions we propose have not been dreamt up in Whitehall, but they come from discussions around the country with the police, local authorities, businesses and families. It is not about waving a magic wand – it is about giving people the tools they need to claim back their communities for the decent law abiding majority.

It is for this reason that we are taking a stand against anti-social behaviour. We will work alongside those who are not prepared to tolerate people harassing and intimidating their neighbours or mistreating our public spaces. We will work with the police, local authorities and schools to ensure that one family is not allowed to ruin a whole street, or one child is not able to disrupt a whole school.

We must be much tougher about forcing people not to behave anti-socially. When people break the rules, there must be consequences for them: consequences that are swift, proportionate and that change the pattern of their behaviour. And where those who are responsible for tackling anti-social behaviour fail to do so, we must intervene. Unless laws are enforced, the signal is clear – if those in a position to act do not do so, then others will not join in. Those who have both the power and the responsibility to act must do so.

Where families and parents are failing to meet their responsibilities to their communities, we will work with them until they do. Where people need our support, we must provide it. Where local people and our public services succeed, we will champion their cause.

Some people say that we are becoming a more selfish society and that we care less for others. I simply do not believe this to be true. The number of people prepared to stand up to anti-social behaviour, outnumber those who make people's lives a misery. In many parts of our country, there are police officers, residents, local authorities, teachers, environmental health officers, neighbourhood wardens and many, many others who are taking a stand and taking action.

We must recognise and build on that, and turn all our communities from places of fear to ones of confidence and safety.

David Blunkett

HOME SECRETARY
March 2003

Contents

Respect and Responsibility – Taking a Stand Against Anti-Social Behaviour

EXECUTIVE SUMMARY

Introduction

Anti-social behaviour means different things to different people – noisy neighbours who ruin the lives of those around them, 'crack houses' run by drug dealers, drunken 'yobs' taking over town centres, people begging by cash-points, abandoned cars, litter and graffiti, young people using airguns to threaten and intimidate or people using fireworks as weapons.

Anti-social behaviour creates an environment in which more serious crime takes hold. It can occur anywhere – in people's homes and gardens, on estates, in town centres or shopping parades and in urban and rural areas. It blights people's lives, undermines the fabric of society and holds back regeneration.

This White Paper is a response to these problems. It outlines the need for a cultural shift from a society where too many people are living with the consequences of anti-social behaviour, to a society where we respect each other, our property and our shared public spaces. Our aim is a society where we have an understanding that the rights we all enjoy are based in turn on the respect and responsibilities we have to other people and to our community.

Crime is something that concerns us all, yet since 1997 overall crime has dropped by over a quarter, and some crimes, such as burglary and vehicle theft, by a third or more. Despite this many people perceive that levels of crime are high and more than one in three people consider that anti-social behaviour has a negative impact on their quality of life.

Family problems, poor educational attainment, unemployment, and alcohol and drug misuse can all contribute to anti-social behaviour. But none of these problems can be used as an excuse for ruining other people's lives. Fundamentally, anti-social behaviour is caused by a lack of respect for other people.

As a society we have rules and standards of behaviour. For the minority who flout these rules and standards, we must take action to enforce them.

To tackle anti-social behaviour we must ensure that:

- Everyone takes responsibility for their own actions and behaves in a way that does not harass or intimidate others.

- Intervention and support is provided to parents and children where their dysfunctional behaviour is ruining other people's lives.

- The community sets clear standards of behaviour. The police, local authorities and others must enforce these standards and take swift, effective action if they are breached.

- The perpetrators of anti-social behaviour are accountable for their actions to those they have affected. We owe a duty to the victims of anti-social behaviour to ensure that they know that perpetrators have been brought to justice.

Building on firm foundations

Since 1997 this Government has put the protection of the community and tackling crime at the heart of its agenda:

- There are now **more police officers** and more police support staff than at any time in history. Tackling anti-social behaviour is firmly embedded as one of four key priorities in the **National Policing Plan** published in November 2002.

- We already have over 1,200 **Community Support Officers (CSOs)** patrolling our streets daily helping to tackle crime and anti-social behaviour. We are on track to meet the target of having over 4,000 CSOs on the streets by the end of 2005.

- Over 240 **neighbourhood warden schemes** are operating in deprived estates bringing safety and peace of mind to many of their residents.

- **Crime and Disorder Reduction Partnerships (CDRPs)** have been established across all local authority and policing areas ensuring that the public can expect their local services to co-ordinate and work together to protect them.

- We have introduced **Anti-Social Behaviour Orders (ASBOs)** to prevent individuals from persisting in behaviour that causes harassment, alarm or distress.

- **Fixed penalty notices (FPNs)** were introduced in 2001 for disorder offences and are being piloted in four areas. An overall payment rate of 60% within 21 days has been achieved. Only 2% end up in court.

- We launched a drive to tackle **street crime** in April 2002 in ten areas, which have seen significant reductions in crime such as robbery and vehicle theft.

These measures have provided the building blocks to tackle anti-social behaviour. Our aim now is to ensure that we deliver further improvements for local people who are being forced to live with anti-social behaviour. And we will ensure that the resources are there to back up this new drive.

Preventing anti-social behaviour – children and families

Strong families are at the centre of peaceful and safe communities. Parents have a critical role in teaching their children the difference between right and wrong, and giving them the confidence to grow up to be proud of themselves, their family, their friends and their community. Respect is all-important, and this is missing in families that behave dysfunctionally.

Early identification of children at risk of committing crime or anti-social behaviour is critical. We will be publishing a Green Paper on Children at Risk in the coming months. It will consider the strategy for universal and targeted provision of services for children. We will also improve support available to parents, through parenting classes and other programmes such as Sure Start and the Children's Fund.

However, some families are unwilling or unable to respond to support when offered it. To address this:

- We will take powers to enable **intensive fostering** to provide an alternative to custody.

- To promote **fostering on remand**, we will introduce a power that allows the court to require local authorities to undertake an initial investigation of the young persons circumstances. The local authority will advise on how it would exercise its responsibilities if the young person is remanded to local authority accommodation.

- Where a child's behaviour is beyond what the parents can cope with in the home, we will support the development of a range of **intensive support schemes** for families.

- We believe that **residential options for parents** experiencing problems to improve their parenting are sometimes needed and will consider whether it is necessary to take further powers to ensure they comply. This may include a residential requirement attached to Parenting Orders.

As well as parents, schools have a key role in tackling anti-social behaviour. We have already introduced action to drive up standards, tackle bad behaviour and truancy. In addition:

- We will give Local Education Authorities (LEAs) and schools powers to ask parents whose children do not attend school regularly or who have been excluded for serious misbehaviour to sign **Parenting Contracts**.

- LEAs will be able to seek a free-standing **Parenting Order** where a child has been excluded for serious misbehaviour.

- Police officers, school and LEA staff will be able to issue a **FPN** to parents who condone or ignore truancy.

We will also strengthen the response to persistent young offenders and reinforce the responsibilities of parents:

- YOTs will be a given a power to issue **Parenting Contracts** to parents of young offenders and to apply to the courts for **Parenting Orders** related to anti-social or criminal behaviour.

- We will consider the issuing of **FPNs to parents**, where their children's behaviour would have warranted action against them, were they to be 16 or over.

- To reduce youth offending still further, the intensive phase of the **Intensive Supervision and Surveillance Programme (ISSP)** will be extended from 6 months to 12 months.

- More than half of all ASBOs are made against 10 to 17 year olds. We will introduce a new **Individual Support Order (ISO)** in the Criminal Justice Bill. This will require children and young people with ASBOs to accept help, such as drug treatment.

Safer and cleaner public places

The effects of anti-social behaviour are most visible in public places. We propose to tackle this by ensuring people feel safer in public spaces, supporting communities to take a stand and tackling environmental crime. These measures include:

- Streamlining existing powers for local authorities to enable them to issue FPNs to people making excessive **noise at night**. Environmental health officers will also to have the power to shut down with immediate effect establishments that persistently create noise nuisance.

- Wholeheartedly supporting a Private Members Bill that will address the abusive use of **fireworks**.

- We will tighten up the gun laws in order to reinforce our strategy to tackle gun crime by introducing new measures on **air weapons and replica guns**.

- New powers to close down **'crack houses'**. Police and local authorities will be given the power to issue notice of impending closure which will enable the property to be closed within 48 hours where Class A drugs are sold and used.

- A new offence of selling **spray paints** to people aged under 18 and, in the Criminal Justice Bill, the police will be given new powers to search for items intended to cause criminal damage.

- We will introduce clearer, more robust powers for local authorities to deal with **fly-tipping, graffiti and fly-posting**.

- The Licensing Bill, currently before Parliament, contains a number of new measures to tackle anti-social behaviour in and around **pubs, clubs and entertainment outlets**. Police will be given a power to close licensed premises within a specified geographical area.

- In addition, guidance will be issued to licensing authorities to make it clear that an application for a new licensed premise could be turned down on the basis that, on police evidence, the **build up of licensed premises** is leading to anti-social behaviour and disorder problems.

- The current offence of **begging** will be made recordable under the National Police Records (Recordable Offences) Regulations 2000 and we will introduce new powers for courts under the Criminal Justice Bill, whereby after three convictions courts will be able to impose a community penalty.

- New style cautions will be introduced for **kerb-crawling** offences and courts will also be able to take away the driving licences of those convicted of kerb-crawling.

Local Problem, Local Action

We cannot achieve success in tackling anti-social behaviour unless local people are part of the solution. It is vital that the right people have the power, the authority and the support to tackle anti-social behaviour.

- **Crime and Disorder Reduction Partnerships** – their strategies will have to fully reflect the action to be taken to address anti-social behaviour locally.

- We have made tackling anti-social behaviour a priority for the **Police** and **Special Constables**.

- There are now more **police officers** than at any time in history and we are on track to reach our target of 132,500 by 2004.

- Every **local authority** has a strategic responsibility under Section 17 of the Crime and Disorder Act 1998 to consider how they can best prevent crime and disorder across all their functions. We will work with local authorities to ensure they meet their responsibilities.

- **Social housing providers** will have more powers to enable them to take action against anti-social tenants including faster evictions and removing their right to buy their council home.

- **Private sector landlords** – new measures will be introduced in the forthcoming Housing Bill that will enable local authorities to target problem private landlords and introduce a licensing scheme.

- **Housing benefit** – we will consult on whether to give local authorities an enabling power to withhold payments of housing benefit to tenants where local authorities believe this is the most effective way of tackling anti-social behaviour.

- **Resident and community groups** – we will continue to encourage local people to become part of the solution by forming residents groups and Neighbourhood Watch schemes.

- **Protecting victims and witnesses** – we will work with the Witness Service, run by Victim Support, to ensure that those giving evidence in ASBO hearings will be able to benefit from the advice and support they provide.

- **Improving court action** – courts will now have to consider the impact of anti-social behaviour on individual victims and the wider community in all housing possession cases.

Effective enforcement

Local authorities, environmental health officers, the police and others have powers that enable them to tackle many forms of anti-social behaviour. Now we need to build on what already works and develop additional tools to tackle the problem.

- **Fixed Penalty Notices (FPNs)** – we will extend the fixed penalty notice scheme to include low-level offences of criminal damage, and also enable notices to be issued to 16-17 year olds, who will be expected to pay their own fines.

- **Fine enforcement** – the overall success rate for the collection of fines is 60%. We will work to improve this and will take contributions directly from salaries or benefits where people have not paid on time.

- **Anti-Social Behaviour Orders (ASBOs)** – we are introducing a range of measures to ensure that ASBOs operate more effectively. We will enable appropriate agencies to access youth court hearings, extend the availability of orders in the County Court, ensure that criminal courts have the information needed to consider an order on conviction, and empower local authorities to prosecute breaches of ASBOs.

- **Community accountability** – we will take measures to improve community accountability. For example, appropriate publicity of action taken is a key part of any strategy to tackle anti-social behaviour: we will lift automatic reporting restrictions on ASBOs on convictions made in the youth court.

- **Restorative justice** ensures that punishment for an offence is accountable and responsive to the wider community. We will be publishing a restorative justice strategy later in the year.

Summary

We must ensure that the rights we share are matched by the responsibilities we owe to each other. As individuals we are responsible for our own actions and we should not behave in a way that intimidates or harasses others. As parents, we are responsible for setting acceptable standards of behaviour and ensuring our children adhere to these standards. As a community we have a responsibility to speak out against the minority who cause misery and distress. Our public servants have a responsibility to use everything in their power to ensure our communities are safe, peaceful and prosperous. It is time to meet our responsibilities and to turn these words into action.

Chapter One

THE TASK AHEAD: BUILDING ON FIRM FOUNDATIONS

1.1   Every society has to have rules and standards of behaviour. Those rules and standards have to be enforced. People who behave anti-socially should not be allowed to get away it with any longer and we believe it is time for the community to take a stand.

1.2   Every community wants young people to be able to socialise with their friends but not to cause trouble or act like thugs; families causing nuisance to be warned, helped but, if necessary, evicted; 'crack houses' to be closed immediately before the dealers wreck the street; people caught doing graffiti to clean it off; people to live free from noise nuisance, families with problems to be given as much help as possible but sanctions applied if their behaviour fails to improve.

1.3   This vision is at the heart of the drive to tackle anti-social behaviour. We know that all around the country there are towns, cities and districts already tackling this problem and doing it well. Our job is to take action where none is being taken, to replicate best practice from around the country and to shift the culture away from protecting the rights of the perpetrator towards protecting the rights of decent people.

1.4   Anti-social behaviour gives rise to fear of crime. Since 1997, the Government has embarked on a drive to combat crime. The results have been positive. Overall crime has dropped by over a quarter.
   - Burglary has dropped 39%
   - Vehicle theft has dropped 32%
   - Violent crime has dropped 26%
   - Since the start of the Street Crime Initiative, street crime has fallen by 16% and by 10% compared with the same period in the previous year.

1.5   But the fear of crime has not fallen to the same extent. And it is fear of crime – rather than actually being a victim – that can so often limit people's lives, making them feel afraid of going out or even afraid in their own homes. The British Crime Survey (BCS) 2001/02 reported that one in three people perceived anti-social behaviour to be a problem in their area. Whilst the media coverage of disturbing crimes can fuel the fear of crime, the real experience of anti-social behaviour and disorder makes many even more afraid of crime.

1.6   Anti-social behaviour means different things to different people. It reflects a range of activities. These include:

- Harassment and intimidating behaviour
- Behaviour that creates alarm or fear
- Noisy neighbours
- Drunken and abusive behaviour
- Vandalism, graffiti and other deliberate damage to property
- Dumping rubbish or litter

1.7   Though there are many different forms of anti-social behaviour, a definition given in the Crime and Disorder Act 1998, is that a 'person has acted in a manner that caused or was likely to cause harassment, alarm or distress to one or more persons not of the same household as himself'. Anti-social behaviour is a problem manifested in hundreds of ways and locations, but the effects of each incident are immediate, real and personal. They can also be long-lasting, causing distress to individuals and sometimes scarring communities for years afterwards.

The spiral of anti-social behaviour

1.8   If a window is broken or a wall is covered in graffiti it can contribute to an environment in which crime takes hold, particularly if intervention is not prompt and effective. An abandoned car, left for days on end, soon becomes a burnt-out car; it is not long before more damage and vandalism takes place. Environmental decline, anti-social behaviour and crime go hand in hand and create a sense of helplessness that nothing can be done.

1.9   The behaviour of a persistent minority can sometimes ruin whole communities. No one should have to put up with behaviour that causes misery and distress. It is time to support the majority against this minority. People need to believe that authorities will help them reclaim their parks from drug dealers, their streets from litter and graffiti and that they can do so without fear of retribution.

1.10   Tackling anti-social behaviour is central to improving people's quality of life. But effective action will not only improve people's quality of life by dealing with the problem, it will also free up the time and resources of those who deal with its consequences. For example, by reducing the number of calls on housing officers to deal with anti-social tenants, on environmental health officers called to noisy neighbour disputes, or on the fire service to put out fires in abandoned vehicles.

Causes

1.11   We all have a responsibility to enforce standards of decent behaviour. If people know where the line is and what happens when they cross it, they are less likely to act anti-socially. Across Government we are also taking action to address the root causes of anti-social behaviour. Key areas are:

Family

- Serious conflict between parents, or between parents and their children is strongly correlated with young people's reported problems at school, drug and alcohol misuse, and anti-social behaviour.
- 80% of children found on truancy sweeps are with an adult.
- There is a very strong correlation between 11-16 year old students reporting family behaviour problems and their own involvement in truancy, exclusion, substance abuse.
- Domestic violence is a pernicious feature in the lives of many families in crisis. It is a crime and its impact on the safety, stability and well being of families is far-reaching. One woman in four will experience domestic violence at some point in their lives.

This White Paper addresses the link between families that are in crisis and anti-social behaviour. The forthcoming Green Paper on Children at Risk will complement this with wider measures for families and children.

Education and employment

- Of approximately 6,000 11-16 year olds in education, almost two thirds of excluded pupils admitted to having committed an offence in the past year. 44% of those who had offended in the past year had also played truant.
- A recent survey of prisoners aged 17-20 found that 21% cannot write their name and address without error. 50% have difficulty telling the time and fewer than a third can complete a job application to a satisfactory standard.
- 75 per cent of males aged 16-17 who are charged and appear before the Youth Court are not in formal full-time activity.

Chapter Two of this White Paper sets out the role that schools and parents can play in tacking anti-social behaviour. The Government has also put major investment into education to give children the best possible start in life.

Deprived areas

- One in ten children are growing up in neglected neighbourhoods marred by drug dealing and other crime where they feel unsafe, especially at night.
- Young people who like and are attached to their communities are significantly less likely to report involvement in problem behaviour than those who want to move elsewhere.

This White Paper is about asking communities to enforce the standards of behaviour they want to see locally. The links to our wider work on community regeneration and neighbourhood renewal are set out in Chapter Four.

Alcohol

- 25% of 'regular drinkers' and 60% of 'binge drinkers' have been involved in criminal and or disorderly behaviour during or after drinking.
- Around one quarter of all incidents of stranger violence occur either in pubs or clubs on Friday, Saturday or Sunday evenings/nights.

The Government's National Alcohol Harm Reduction Strategy consultation period closed at the beginning of March and a final report is due to be published this summer. The Licensing Bill is also currently before Parliament. Chapter Three shows how these will help us tackle anti-social behaviour.

Drugs

- The areas with the highest rates of acquisitive crime (burglary, theft and shoplifting) are the same areas that have higher drugs misuse problems.
- One in three people feel that drug use or dealing is a very or fairly big problem in their local area.

The National Drugs Strategy was updated in November 2002. It sets out a range of policies and interventions that focus on the most dangerous drugs, the most damaged communities and the individuals whose addiction and chaotic lifestyles are most harmful to themselves and everyone around them. The Government's spending will rise from a planned £1.026 billion in this financial year to £1.244 billion in the next financial year, rising to a total annual spend of nearly £1.5 billion in the year starting April 2005. Over 9,000 drug treatment and testing orders were granted between October 2000 and September 2002.

Rights and Responsibilities

1.12 The common element in all anti-social behaviour is that it represents a lack of respect or consideration for other people. It shows a selfish inability or unwillingness to recognise when one's individual behaviour is offensive to others, and a refusal to take responsibility for it. More fundamentally it shows a failure to understand that one person's rights are based on the responsibilities we have towards others and towards our families and our communities.

1.13 Effective enforcement is key. There must be a consistent message that sanctions against anti-social behaviour are extremely serious and that breach of them will lead to unwelcome consequences for the perpetrators.

1.14 This is a web of rights and responsibilities that involves the whole of society; every individual and every community. Communities need to be empowered and everyone must play their part in setting and enforcing standards of behaviour:

- **The role of individuals, families, communities and businesses** is to get involved and take responsibility. Parents are responsible for ensuring that their children attend school and are supported in their learning. Citizens have the responsibility for being part of the criminal justice system through jury service. Witnesses of crime have a responsibility to give evidence and a right to feel secure in doing so. Businesses must do the simple things like removing or paying for the removal of rubbish from outside their premises. And together we must support public services to tackle anti-social behaviour. In many parts of the country residents, tenants and other groups are doing just this.

- **The role of public services, local authorities, social services, teachers and the police** is to discourage and prevent anti-social behaviour, to stop it when it happens and deal with its consequences on behalf of the rest of society. It is important that public services are accountable to the broader community as well as delivering services to the individual clients. And anti-social behaviour cannot be left to specialist agencies to tackle. Too often, the police and the local authority housing department, are expected to provide all the response that is needed. While both are essential, other agencies must recognise their responsibilities. The youth service, Connexions, social services, schools, environmental health departments all need to share responsibility for tackling the anti-social behaviour of those with whom they are working. We will expect local partners, through Crime and Disorder Reduction Partnerships (CDRPs), to fully reflect the action they are taking on anti-social behaviour in their strategies.

- **The role of Government** is to set out the framework and provide leadership, tools and resources to ensure that local agencies and communities can deliver the new approach. The Government will publish a Bill of new measures to strengthen the tools available to the police, local authorities, environmental health officers and local communities to deal with anti-social behaviour. Their role will be vital as we target both the places and the people where anti-social behaviour is a problem. Many of the proposals in this White Paper have been suggested by local authorities who are in the frontline in tackling anti-social behaviour. Many will, over time, save money. But where new responsibilities bring new costs we will ensure there are resources available.

Building on firm foundations

1.15   The foundations for the action set out in this White Paper have been well established over the last six years. All Government departments have played their part. The key strategic elements that the Home Office have put in place are:

A new system of orders and penalties

1.16   One of the Government's first actions was to introduce the Crime and Disorder Act 1998 to tackle crime and disorder and create safer communities. The Act brought together the police and local authorities, with other agencies and the wider community, in Crime and Disorder Reduction Partnerships (CDRPs), to produce comprehensive strategies to respond to locally identified crime and disorder problems.

1.17   The 1998 Act created ASBOs to protect the public from behaviour that causes or is likely to cause harassment, alarm or distress. These are civil orders issued by magistrates and, since last year, criminal courts can prohibit offenders from carrying out specific acts or entering specific areas for a minimum of two years.

1.18   For the first time, ASBOs gave the police and courts proper powers to address anti-social behaviour. ASBOs are an effective method of tackling low level nuisance like vandalism, stone-throwing and general abusive behaviour. Up and down the country they are now being used by local authorities and the police.

1.19   The procedure for obtaining ASBOs was streamlined by the Police Reform Act 2002, which have been supplemented by non-statutory Acceptable Behaviour Contracts (ABCs) pioneered by local authorities. Guidance on ASBOs and ABCs with good practice examples was published by the Home Office in November 2002. There are over 170 ABC schemes across England and Wales.

1.20　The Crime and Disorder 1998 Act also introduced:

- Parenting Orders to compel those parents who do not take responsibility for their children's behaviour to do so. Between April 2000 and April 2002, almost 2,200 orders had been issued by the courts.

1.21　The Criminal Justice and Police Act 2001 also introduced a range of measures relating to law enforcement, many of which were relevant to anti-social behaviour, including:

- introducing FPNs for disorderly offending
- restricting drinking in certain public places
- closing disorderly licensed or unlicensed premises
- making it a criminal offence to intimidate or harm witnesses in civil proceedings
- making kerb crawling an arrestable offence

1.22　The Police Reform Act 2002 contained measures to enhance the effectiveness of ASBOs, and extended the police family to support the police in dealing with low level crime and anti-social behaviour, including:

- introducing interim ASBOs as well as giving criminal courts the power to issue an ASBO on conviction of a criminal offence and County Courts the power to issue ASBOs alongside related proceedings, such as housing possession;

- enabling the British Transport Police and registered social landlords to apply for ASBOs;

- extending the area an ASBO can cover to any defined part, or the whole of England and Wales;

- providing for Chief Officers of Police to designate support staff as Community Support Officers with powers to clamp down on anti-social behaviour;

- measures to regulate the use of off-road vehicles, including confiscation of such vehicles

The National Policing Plan

1.23　Tackling anti-social behaviour is one of the Government's four key national policing priorities. This is the first time anti-social behaviour has been made a priority for the police. The

National Policing Plan, published in November 2002, set out the actions which Chief Officers of Police and police authorities should take at a local level to support the delivery of this key priority. Chief Officers and police authorities, working with local Crime and Disorder Reduction Partnerships, should include in their local plans a strategy for tackling youth nuisance and anti-social behaviour, covering all aspects of the local problem. They should make full use of the range of existing powers and use officers, special constables, and Community Support Officers to help address the problem. Police forces are also encouraged to adopt, wherever possible, a problem solving approach in their response to anti-social behaviour.

The Street Crime Initiative

1.24   The Street Crime Initiative was launched in April 2002 in the ten police force areas with the highest rates of recorded robbery during 2001-02. Its key aims are to increase the detection rate for street crime cases, increase the proportion of offenders charged and brought to justice, and speed up the process between arrest and sentence.

1.25   This practical and partnership driven approach from the Government, police and other agencies had, by the end of September 2002, reduced the overall number of street crime offences by 16%.

Measures against football hooliganism

1.26   The Government has worked closely with the police, football authorities and supporter groups to tackle hooliganism. Our grounds are now as safe and secure as any in the world and more families are attending matches. However, the hooligans may be fewer in number but can still cause problems. That is why Government introduced tough new legislation (Football (Disorder) Act 2000) which prevents known troublemakers from attending domestic and international matches for up to 10 years.

The task ahead

1.27   Although there is a wide range of measures in place to address anti-social behaviour, it is clear from what we know and from what people tell us that more remains to be done to address their concerns.

Chapter Two

FAMILIES, CHILDREN AND YOUNG PEOPLE: PREVENTING ANTI-SOCIAL BEHAVIOUR AND PROTECTING COMMUNITIES

2.1   Healthy communities are built on strong families. These are communities where people know their neighbours and can call on them in good times and in bad. These are neighbourhoods that are safe, where parents take responsibility for their children's well being and behaviour, where parents are confident in bringing up their children, and know there are good schools and good services.

2.2   Parents have to set limits; they have to ensure their children understand the difference between right and wrong. Without this children feel free to do as they wish and can, in some cases, make life a misery for everybody. The most important influence in a child's life is their family and friends but teachers, the police and other professionals have a role to play in early prevention of anti-social behaviour. Strong families teach values, provide stability, offer the support that children need, and protect them physically and emotionally.

Green Paper on Children at Risk

In the coming months the Government will publish a Green Paper on Children at Risk, which will propose radical options to improve services for children who are at risk of a wide range of poor outcomes. These outcomes include anti-social behaviour and offending; educational underachievement; abuse, neglect and victimisation; teenage pregnancy; and ill health.

The Green Paper will set out how families and communities can offer the best possible support to children and young people and how we will identify children and young people at risk. Building on recent developments in children's services we will set out proposals on effective interventions; on tackling the current difficulties in the workforce; and on ensuring the underpinning structures support co-ordinated service delivery.

Young People

2.3   Young people are more often the victims of crime and anti-social behaviour than the perpetrators. Parents and families can usually cope with the normal problems and challenges of growing children or if a problem becomes more serious, are very willing to work with others to deal with it.

2.4   A key priority for Government is to improve the co-ordination of services for children and young people at risk. In 2002, we announced that all local authorities would have to develop local preventative strategies and last autumn we published interim guidance. Chief Executives are being asked to take the lead in ensuring that all partners agree a local preventative strategy from April 2003.

2.5   A new Identification, Referral and Tracking system (IRT) is being developed across all services working with children to enable a speedier and more joined up response to problems and is already being piloted in 10 areas in England. The development of IRT will enable all agencies to share information about young people at risk. It will mean, for example, that when a young person who is committing anti-social behaviour comes to the attention of the police, this information will be shared with schools, social services, the youth service and other agencies who may be working with them. We expect all these agencies to include action to tackle the offending behaviour as a key part of their work with that young person.

2.6   In recognition that there can be structural barriers to improving the co-ordination of services for children and young people, the Government is piloting Children's Trusts. These will provide the opportunity for local authorities and Primary Care Trusts to work in an integrated way with other organisations to plan, commission and deliver services for children and young people.

2.7   Children's Trusts are just one of a number of ways we can achieve better co-ordination of services at a local level. The Green Paper on Children at Risk to be published in the coming months will consider further the broader strategy for universal and targeted provision. It will look at what further measures are needed, at how clear national standards can be established and how local services will be held accountable for their achievement. This will develop a long-term approach that draws in the local public services, voluntary sector and, most importantly, the capacity and strengths of broader social support networks.

Family Support

2.8   All parents and families experience problems. Extended family members, friends and the wider community are often able to give support and advice. But sometimes this is not enough or not available. Helplines, such as the 24-hour free service provided by Parentline Plus, or befriending and home visiting services can be vital in bridging the gap and preventing problems escalating.

2.9   There are a small number of families that can be described as 'dysfunctional'. Two or three families and their wider network of contacts can create havoc on a housing estate or inner city neighbourhood. It is always in areas of greatest disadvantage that this corrosive effect is seen and felt most clearly. Sometimes it occurs where there has been considerable family breakdown; multiple partners can pass through the house; children do not have a positive role model; there is little in the way of predictable orderly routine; and the lifestyle is such that it makes the lives of neighbours a complete misery. Some professionals have refrained from demanding changes in standards and behaviour from such families, in an effort to remain 'non-judgmental'. This stance alienates those living alongside chaotic families and who legitimately complain that professionals can go home to areas not beset by this kind of misery. It also fails children in dysfunctional families by not asserting their need for care and discipline by their parents.

2.10   Parenting classes are critical in supporting parents to feel confident in establishing and maintaining a sense of responsibility, decency and respect in their children, and in helping parents manage them. This work is reinforced by the ideas and values that young people learn in citizenship and Personal, Social and Health Education (PSHE) at school.

2.11   A Parenting Fund of £25m, announced in 2002, has also been established to deliver early help to parents. This money will be used to provide a variety of services, including parenting classes and workshops, community based family centres and support, parenting helplines and home visiting services.

2.12   Early years, childcare services and health visitors provide support to parents of young children. Parents often receive indirect support from other front line professionals such as teachers and GPs. Equally important are services such as learning mentors and learning support units (operating outside the classroom) which work with teachers, pupils and their parents to ensure that barriers which prevent learning are overcome and keep children in education by providing extra support for their learning needs, rather than excluding them.

2.13   We are developing a Children's National Service Framework to set out national standards for health and social services and consider how best to support families through these services.

2.14   After school clubs, extended schools, the youth service and local sports and arts schemes can all provide positive opportunities for children and young people outside traditional school hours.

Parents needing more support

2.15   Universal services like GPs are the gateway into more specialist services for parents and carers who need extra support; for example, when a child is starting to have serious problems in schools, to misuse drugs or alcohol or committing anti-social or criminal behaviour. We have made considerable investment in delivering targeted support to parents whose children may be at greatest risk of problems, including anti-social behaviour. Programmes such as Sure Start and the Children's Fund were set up to deliver preventative services to children and families. Sure Start works in disadvantaged communities, but with all parents in the area. The Children's Fund focuses on those between 5-13, when young people experience major challenges such as moving from primary to secondary education. It aims to support children within the home, school and community, and supports parents so children can achieve their ambitions.

On Track projects (now part of the Children's Fund) have a specific focus on a set of evidence based services for parents and families for reducing delinquency in children aged 4-12. Each On Track project is based in a community about the size of a secondary school catchment area.

Solihull On Track's services include:

- Parent support group and training – delivered at the NCH Smith's Wood Family Partnership Centre
- Family Therapy – solution-focused family therapy delivered by a social worker and systemic therapy delivered through CAMHS
- Home School partnerships – a primary drop-in service and education unit has been supporting children who are showing difficulties at school
- Home Visiting – provided by NCH Smith's Wood Family Partnership Centre

2.16   At the local level Youth Offending Teams (YOTs) have been running parenting classes for parents whose children are starting to get into trouble with the police, both on a voluntary basis and for those who have a Parenting Order. The Youth Justice Board (YJB) evaluation indicates that the Parenting Order contributed to a 50% reduction in reconviction rates in children whose parents take up classes. Many of the parents would like to have been offered help years earlier. We want the benefits of parenting support to be an option for more parents on a voluntary basis in the first instance, through Parenting Contracts. We will also ensure that we have mechanisms for parents who are not willing to address their child's behaviour and we will be increasing the circumstances in which Parenting Orders can be made.

In 2002-3, **Parentline Plus** aim to reach over 3000 parents and carers with workshops and courses designed to develop their skills, confidence and enjoyment of parenting, and to promote social networks. The workshops are funded from the Nationwide Foundation, and by local authorities, schools, local trusts and foundations, Sure Start projects and Youth Offending Teams.

Family Links is an independent, Oxford based charity set up in 1994. Between September and December 2002, 50 Parenting Classes were run (each involving 10 parents) by Family Links trained leaders. The leaders also use materials provided by Family Links and are supervised by them.

C'mon Everybody is an organisation based in Sheffield started up with Home Office funding. The team aims to provide a flexible service supporting the needs of families and children working with schools and nurseries, GPs, Sure Start, School Nurses, Family Support Workers, Play Workers. C'mon Everybody helps parents develop positive interactions with their children, through a mix of videotape modelling and therapist led group discussion.

Homestart is a voluntary organisation supporting families with significant difficulties where there is at least one child under five through home visiting and reconnecting families with their communities. In 2001/02, Home-Start's work has benefited some 54,000 children in 24,000 families, using 8,700 volunteers across the UK.

2.17   The Government believes Family Group Conferencing (FGC) can be an effective way of dealing with offending behaviour. For example, since 1999, the Essex Family Group Conference Service has developed the use of FGCs with young offenders. 91% of those victims who attended were happy with the outcome of the conference. The rate of re-offending is low – in the first year of the project only 31% of offenders who had an FGC have re-offended.

2.18   Some families also need access to services such as child mental health workers, specialist learning support and tailored drug treatment for young people. The Government recognises the pressure on these services and the Green Paper on Children at Risk will set out proposals to strengthen provision across the country.

Families and communities in crisis

2.19   Some families are unwilling or unable to respond to support when offered it. In every neighbourhood where there is anti-social behaviour local people will know the small number of families who are at the root of so much of it. They are often the families who cause the most noise, whose children do not attend school on a regular basis or if they do, cause trouble.

2.20   These families require specialist, intensive and long-term support tailored to their particular needs. These needs may relate to serious difficulties and deficiencies in parenting, problems with alcohol and drugs misuse, domestic violence, mental illness or a parent in prison. In some cases we will need to bring in the full force of the law to prevent abuse and violence in the family. For example, in the updated National Drugs Strategy published in December 2002, the Government set out how it will provide more support to parents, carers and families so that they can easily access advice, help, counselling and mutual support. Often families need some practical assistance in managing their children and household budget.

- In households where there is domestic violence and children under the age of 16, 29% of children were witnesses and when the violence was extreme, 45% of children were witnesses.

- 60% of child protection case conferences found that heavy drinking parents were a contributory factor to those proceedings.

- It is estimated that each year 125,000 children are affected by the imprisonment of a parent.

2.21   Given the complexity of these problems, it is essential that support is properly co-ordinated and targeted; mechanisms between agencies need to ensure that intervention is strong, persistent and holds the family to account whilst also engaging the local community. We will address this in the Green Paper on Children at Risk .

Intensive family support including fostering

2.22   For some parents, their child's behaviour is beyond what they can cope with in the home, even with the support of skilled professionals. We will encourage the development of an increased range of specialised, high quality intensive support schemes to help these parents and children in order to implement more effectively the Children Act 1989 provisions. These schemes will better support families where a lack of parental capacity or ability contributes significantly to the child's behavioural problems.

2.23   In some such cases placing a child away from the family home, whether temporarily or longer term, can improve the child's future. This will provide the best opportunity for a child to develop in a setting where they can have the necessary support to which they are entitled and to develop a clear sense of responsibility for their own behaviour.

2.24   We will be taking powers to enable intensive fostering to occur as an alternative to custody. Intensive fostering requires support from a range professionals with the right skills to address the full range of young people's needs such as mental ill-health, drug and alcohol misuse and low educational attainment. At the same time it is essential to work with the family to enhance their parenting skills with a view to the child returning home.

> **ROSTA**
>
> The ROSTA project in Liverpool provides therapeutic fostering for 12-17 year olds with complex needs. An inter-agency, multi-disciplinary team provides therapeutic foster care with intensive support and clinical supervision, individual and family therapy, systemic consultation, individual and group-based day programme, educational re-integration, psychiatric consultation and a 24-hour support worker service.

2.25   We are also keen to explore how other models of family support, such as 'support foster care', could be developed to help young people and their families.

Birmingham City Council's Neighbourhood Support Scheme is an affordable, alternative means of maintaining children from problem families within their own community.
- The scheme provides children aged up to 8 with short breaks away from home to relieve family tension, helping to prevent periods of more formal accommodation which can be expensive, traumatic and damaging to family relationships.
- Parents are able to make positive links with their local community, preventing social isolation.
- Positive attitudes towards the long-term health and education needs of children in placement are promoted, and support packages are developed as appropriate to the needs of individual families. Referrals are usually responded to within 5 days, and placements are contractual, with clear guidelines in place for all parties.

In 2000-01, 86 children were placed as a result of referrals from social workers, but also from health visitors, outreach workers and family support units.

2.26   Young people can currently be fostered on remand, provided they are remanded to local authority accommodation. However, it is not often taken up as courts do not have the confidence that fostering will be an option. We will introduce a power that allows the court to require local authorities to undertake an initial investigation of the young person's circumstances and advise on how it would exercise its responsibilities should the young person be remanded to local authority accommodation. This will facilitate dialogue between courts and local authorities, and we will encourage, through guidance, fostering to be taken up as a remand option where this is deemed appropriate.

2.27   In some cases it is necessary to work intensively with the family as a whole. We will look to build on existing 'homemaking' provision in the voluntary and statutory sectors where support is provided directly to the family, in their homes. This might include support and guidance, as well as helping families to manage day-to-day tasks.

Family Welfare Association (FWA) Home Based Family Support

The purpose of FWA Home Based Family Support is to reduce the involvement of children and young people in crime, juvenile nuisance and anti-social activities, which put themselves, their families or communities at risk. The project works with children and their families together, as the children are likely to be behaving badly due to poor parenting.

2.28   Where parental and parenting problems are having an impact on their child's development, other options would be to work with parents in residential settings such as residential family centres or building on innovative voluntary sector projects such as the Dundee Families Project run by NCH Action for Children. We hope that families who are at the stage where only drastic action will work will accept such support voluntarily. Where the family is in serious crisis and help is it not accepted, the children are very likely to be at risk.

The **Dundee Families Project** works with families deemed to have exhibited a range of anti-social behaviour. It provides a systemic approach to family difficulties and offers a range of services through individual and couple counselling, family support and group work. Support is available 24 hours a day. Staff run after-school and young persons' activities, while groups for adults have covered cookery, parenting skills, anger management and tenancy issues. Users access the service in three main ways;
- By residence
- In dispersed tenancies
- On an outreach basis

2.29   Whilst we want to address anti-social behaviour by tackling the problems in families that lie behind it, we should be in no doubt that communities cannot be expected to suffer nuisance, disorder, damage and harassment for month after month. So positive work with families must always be allied to a clear understanding – by professional agencies and the perpetrators – that the protection of communities must come first. We expect that professional agencies will be prepared to make it clear that they will use a range of criminal and civil sanctions to secure the co-operation of families in tackling anti-social behaviour. If the situation is putting the children or broader community at severe risk, the courts can remove the children from the home or move the whole family out of the neighbourhood. We will consider whether we need to take further powers to ensure parents comply, for example by extending a Parenting Order to include a residential requirement. If the parents refuse to comply in tackling anti-social behaviour, other legal remedies are available, including ASBOs and injunctions. We are also introducing measures to make it easier for anti-social tenants to be evicted; these are set out in Chapter Four.

Schools

2.30   Schools have a pivotal role in tackling anti-social behaviour. Education is a key determinant of aspirations and life chances of young people. The Government's continuing drive to raise standards in schools has a crucial part to play in preventing anti-social behaviour. There are strong links between poor education and future offending behaviour. We are working with schools and Local Education Authorities (LEAs) to:

- raise educational standards for all children and young people
- support children and young people who are struggling

- improve behaviour in schools
- tackle truancy
- reinforce parental support and responsibility for their children's education.

2.31 In autumn 2002, 'Citizenship' became part of the secondary National Curriculum. This will give young people the knowledge, skills and understanding to play an effective role in the community, and be aware of their rights and responsibilities. It aims to make young people more self-confident and responsible in and beyond the classroom and encourages them to play a helpful part in their schools, communities and the wider world. The Office for Standards in Education (Ofsted) will monitor this process

2.32 Mentoring involving young people as peers is useful in promoting tolerance and helping young people understand the effects of anti-social behaviour, and provide positive role models for young people rather than the negative impact of some peer groups and gangs. It also help build confidence in young people affected by bullying and anti-social behaviour. The Department for Education and Skills (DfES) anti-bullying pack for schools provides guidance on these approaches.

2.33 We have launched a wide-ranging programme of measures to tackle bad behaviour and truancy. Over the next three years we will be investing nearly £470 million in a National Behaviour and Attendance Strategy, which will have two elements:

- A universal element providing consultancy support, audits and behaviour training for all secondary schools. It will help to ensure that senior managers have a clear strategy for behaviour and attendance management and teachers are more confident about managing behaviour in the classroom.
- A targeted element for schools facing more serious problems. In April 2002, we launched Behaviour Improvement Projects (BIPs) – tailored packages of measures to support selected schools in the 34 LEAs with the highest levels of street crime and truancy. BIPs include key workers to support children at risk of truancy or exclusion from school and Behaviour and Education Support Teams to provide multi-agency support for children with the most serious problems. Over the summer, they also provided key workers and positive activities for over 10,000 young people most at risk of committing crime. By 2005-06 BIPs will be extended to 61 LEAs and 89 Excellence Clusters, providing intensive support for about 400 secondary schools and about 1,500 primary schools educating about 800,000 children.

2.34 Parents have a legal responsibility for ensuring that their children behave in an acceptable way and attend school regularly. The great majority of parents live up to these responsibilities, but some do not. We therefore propose to give LEAs and schools formal powers to ask parents who have failed to secure their child's regular attendance or whose child has been excluded for serious misbehaviour to sign Parenting Contracts. By signing the contract, parents will be required to co-operate with support provided or arranged by the LEA or the school (such as parenting classes) and to take specified action to improve their child's attendance or behaviour.

2.35 Parents may be told that refusal to sign or breach of the contract will result in a fixed penalty notice or prosecution (for an attendance related contract) or a court-imposed Parenting Order (for an exclusion related contract).

2.36 Existing legislation enables courts to impose a Parenting Order where parents have been convicted because of their child's truancy. To complement this provision we propose to enable LEAs to seek a freestanding Parenting Order where a child has been excluded for serious misbehaviour. If LEAs judge that an exclusion-related parenting contract is not likely to be effective they will be able to apply for a Parenting Order immediately.

2.37 We propose to provide an alternative to prosecution by enabling designated LEA and school staff and police officers to issue FPNs to parents who condone or ignore truancy.

2.38 The DfES is working with twenty-two LEAs acting as pathfinders for a fast-track prosecution for truancy. The aim of the fast track approach is to make the prosecution process more streamlined by setting a court date at the beginning of a fixed period during which LEAs work with parents to bring about an improvement in the attendance of their children. The aim is to extend the scheme nationally from September 2003.

The Youth Service and Connexions

CONNEXIONS

Connexions personal advisers help young people identify and overcome the barriers they face, brokering appropriate support and provision. For those under 16 this is done in close partnership with the school and local authority. By doing this, Connexions can play an important part in preventing anti-social behaviour. However, when a young person starts behaving anti-socially personal advisers can:

- Broker alternative curriculum solutions for those whose behavioural problems are linked to school;
- Work with the Educational Welfare Service and police in dealing with young people picked up as a result of truancy sweeps, providing them with targeted support on re-engaging and staying engaged in education;
- Work with Safer Schools Partnerships in identification of young people at risk of offending; and
- Play a key worker role in ensuring young people who have participated in positive activities in the summer are supported back into education, training or employment.

2.40   We know that when young people have diversionary activities to keep them occupied anti-social behaviour and crime are often reduced. The Youth Service plays a key role in engaging young people in their communities. LEAs are responsible for the Youth Service in their area and work in partnership with the voluntary and community sector to deliver a wide range of services. This provides learning and challenge through constructive activities that are built around the interests of individuals and the issues they face.

WEST YORKSHIRE PLAYHOUSE

Detached youth workers in Leeds used their outreach work to attract young people to activities provided by the **West Yorkshire Playhouse** in Summer 2002. Activities included video production, DJ-ing and graffiti artwork. An outdoor skateboard ramp and giant games such as Jenga and Connect4 were also installed on-site. The Playhouse was used for 3-4 days at a time during each week of the summer holidays. A number of drama workshops were also held inside the theatre accommodation.

2.41   These activities depend quite often on volunteers and in return for wanting safer streets and lower crime in their neighbourhood everyone has a part to play in partnership with the authorities – giving time to work with young people is a positive contribution.

Operation Garden City in Wythenshawe is a multi-agency initiative aimed at tackling youth nuisance. It involves high visibility policing and an extensive programme of youth activities. This means that when police are called to an incident of youth nuisance they are able to have a positive impact on young people by offering alternatives to hanging around the streets. The operation has led to a 40% reduction in youth nuisance and 19% reduction in crime overall.

Street Crime Initiatives

Summer activities provided by Youth Offending Teams, Connexions, Youth Services and community and voluntary sports and arts groups have been an integral part of the Government's drive to tackle street crime. Results from programmes run in summer 2002 were impressive.
- Robbery in Connexions Summer Plus areas declined by 9% compared with the previous quarter.
- Total crime around areas where the Splash Extra scheme ran in summer 2002 decreased by 5.2% during the period July to September 2002.
- The six Police Force Areas for which comparative data was available for July and August 2002 and 2001 all showed significant reductions in robbery within areas covered by Splash Extra, of between 9% and 31%.

2.42 Government Departments are bringing together funding for summer/diversionary activities into a single pot. This work has culminated in the launch of a new programme of positive activities for young people. Activities will be available across the country for all holiday periods, with the focus on crime hotspots, Behaviour Improvement Programme schools and community cohesion areas. It involves a comprehensive programme of quality sports, arts, creative and personal development activities for young people. Key workers played a pivotal role last year for those targeted under the Connexions Summer Plus Programme. The key worker ensures that each young person receives a tailored package of provision and is supported back into education, training or employment.

Other activities for young people
- The Youth Justice Board's Youth Inclusion Programme focuses on the 50 most at risk young people aged 13-16 on 70 of the most deprived/high crime estates in England and Wales. Latest figures show there has been a very substantial reduction – of some 66% – in arrest rates for the 'top 50' who were actively engaged in the Youth Inclusion Programme in the quarter to June 2002.
- Positive Futures projects operate in 67 of the country's most deprived wards and neighbourhoods. They use sport to reduce anti-social behaviour, crime and drug misuse. They target the 50 most vulnerable young people aged 10-16 within the selected neighbourhood. The programmes are delivered by a range of agencies including local authorities, charities, sports clubs and crime reduction agencies.

Having the right powers and means to deal with anti-social behaviour

2.43   Much of our framework aims to prevent anti-social behaviour; and where influencing, supporting and negotiation fail we need the right powers to take effect swiftly to ensure compliance and to protect the broader community.

2.44   In some cases parents are not willing to engage voluntarily. Parenting Orders are currently available (in non-education proceedings) when a child is convicted of an offence in court, or when they receive an ASBO, Sex Offender Order or a Child Safety Order. This is often once anti-social and offending behaviour has become entrenched. We want to empower YOTs to take action at an earlier stage. We therefore propose to take powers to enable YOTs to apply to the courts for Parenting Orders related to anti-social or criminal type behaviour in the community where the parent is not taking active steps to prevent the child's behaviour, and it is clear that the behaviour will continue. These arrangements will complement those for freestanding Parenting Orders for bad behaviour in schools. The work of YOTs should fully reflect the needs of the wider community, and not solely those of the individual with whom they are working.

2.45   We also want to ensure that support is provided for parents of young people with ASBOs. At the moment, courts can make a Parenting Order when making an ASBO but this power is rarely used – between June 2000 and December 2001 only nine Parenting Orders were made in this way – whereas more than 200 ASBOs were granted against juveniles in the same period. That is why we will place an obligation on a court to consider a Parenting Order where a person under the age of 16 has been given an ASBO.

Strengthening the response to persistent young offenders

2.46   For some young people anti-social behaviour, if unchecked, will go on to become serious and persistent offending. In 2001 there were 25,393 persistent young offenders in England and Wales sentenced in magistrates and crown courts. They are responsible for a disproportionate amount of crime and disorder in their neighbourhood. The Intensive Supervision and Surveillance Programme (ISSP) is one of the most rigorous community based interventions available for the most prolific and serious young offenders and provides a credible alternative to the use of secure remands and custodial sentences. ISSP combines community based surveillance with a comprehensive and sustained focus on tackling the factors that contribute to the young person's offending behaviour. It is available for those on bail, subject to a community sentence or for those young offenders on the community phase of the Detention and Training Order.

2.47 We want to develop ISSP further to make it a simpler and tougher measure and improve its effectiveness. Currently the programme is only available for 6 months and there are some young offenders who require longer and more intensive programmes. As a result, we will be extending ISSP to allow it to be available for up to 12 months as part of a Supervision Order.

2.48 More than half of all ASBOs are made against 10 to 17 year olds yet the courts do not have any powers to require a young person with an ASBO to address their anti-social behaviour. To ensure that this support is provided the Government is introducing an innovative new Individual Support Order (ISO) within the Criminal Justice Bill. The new order will extend the protection that ASBOs provide to the community by requiring children and young people with ASBOs to undertake individually tailored activities. They may, for example, be required to attend treatment for substance abuse. This will improve the effectiveness of an ASBO by engaging the child or young person in addressing the root causes of their actions and aiming to solve these problems.

2.49 To reinforce the drive to get parents to take responsibility for their children, we will consider the issuing of FPNs to parents, where their children's behaviour would otherwise have warranted action against them, were they to have been 16 or over.

2.50 The Criminal Justice and Police Act 2001 strengthened secure remand powers for 12-16 year olds and introduced tagging on bail.

2.51 In this chapter we have set out a range of measures to support families and young people who are involved in anti-social activity in order to change their behaviour. We have also set out strong sanctions against such behaviour. In the past some agencies have picked and chosen whether they want to be involved in support or sanctions. It is important that in order to create safe and secure communities for everyone all organisations in any local area need to follow a consistent principle – that the protection of the local community must come first.

CHAPTER TWO: SUMMARY OF NEW MEASURES

Young People

- The Green Paper on Children at Risk to be published in the coming months will consider further the broader strategy for universal and targeted provision of services for children. It will look at what further measures are needed, at how clear national standards can be established and how local services will be held accountable for their achievement.

Parents needing more support

- We will be increasing the number of parents who take up parenting classes on a voluntary basis, and also ensuring that we have mechanisms to ensure parents comply, such as taking the statutory powers to make Parenting Contracts and increasing the circumstances in which Parenting Orders can be made.

Families and communities in crisis

- We will encourage the development of an increased range of specialised, high quality intensive support schemes to help Parents and Children and more effectively implement the Children Act 1989.

- We will take powers so that intensive fostering can be provided as an alternative to custody.

- To promote fostering on remand, we will introduce a power that allows the court to require local authorities to undertake an initial investigation of the young person's circumstances. The local authority will advise on how it would exercise its responsibilities should the young person be remanded to local authority accommodation.

- We will consider whether we need to take further powers where necessary, for example by extending a Parenting Order to include a residential requirement.

- We will look to build on existing home-making provision in the voluntary and statutory sectors where support is provided directly to the family in their home.

- We will consider how best to streamline the number of authorities that work with chaotic families at anyonetime, so that intervention is intensive and co-ordinated. We will set out details on this in the Green Paper on Children at Risk .

Schools

- We will give Local Education Authorities (LEAs) and schools powers to ask parents who have failed to secure their child's regular attendance or whose child has been excluded for serious misbehaviour to sign parenting contracts.

- Refusal to sign or breach of the contract may result in a fixed penalty notice or prosecution (for an attendance-related contract) or a court imposed Parenting Order (for an exclusion-related contract).

- Designated LEA and school staff and police officers will have powers to issue FPNs to parents who condone or ignore truancy.

- We will enable LEAs to seek a free-standing Parenting Order where a child has been excluded for serious misbehaviour

Having the right powers

- Youth Offending Teams (YOTs) will be able to work with parents whose children are at risk of offending using Parenting Contracts.

- YOTs will be able to apply to the courts for Parenting Orders related to anti-social or criminal type behaviour in the community where the parent is not taking active steps to prevent the child's behaviour, and it is clear that the behaviour will continue.

- We will place an obligation on a court to consider a Parenting Order where a person under the age of 16 has been given an ASBO.

Strengthening the response

- The Intensive Supervision and Surveillance Programme (ISSP) is the most rigorous community based intervention available for the most prolific and serious young offenders and provides a credible alternative to the use of secure remands and custodial sentences. We will make ISSP a simpler and tougher measure and improve its effectiveness.

- To ensure that this support is provided the government is introducing an innovative new Individual Support Order (ISO) within the Criminal Justice Bill. This will require children and young people with ASBOs to accept help, such as drug treatment where appropriate.

- We will consider the issuing of FPNs to parents, where their children's behaviour would otherwise have warranted action against them were they to have been 16 or over.

Chapter Three

SAFER AND CLEANER PUBLIC PLACES

3.1 The effects of anti-social behaviour are most visible when the results of that behaviour ruin public places such as shopping precincts, parks, playgrounds, town centres or railway stations. It can also degrade local areas by allowing gardens, homes and streets to be full of litter and rubbish.

3.2 Unfortunately there are some people or families whose intimidating and aggressive behaviour ruins people's lives. We need to take action against this small minority, but the public as a whole also has an obligation to treat our public spaces with respect.

3.3 Places that are neglected encourage more graffiti, littering and vandalism. This in turn undermines public confidence, leads people to avoid them and gives way to crime. There is also a major drain on the public purse – the estimated cost of cleaning up graffiti in London alone is £23 million every year.

3.4 There are two elements to the Government's drive to tackle anti social behaviour in public places:

- **Enforcing local standards and tackling the abuse of our environment** that make public places a magnet for anti-social behaviour and crime.

- Tackling the **intimidating and offensive behaviour** that disrupts the lives of decent citizens and ensuring that enforcement agencies have quick and effective means of dealing with problems.

Enforcing local standards and tackling the abuse of our environment

Noise nuisance

3.5   Some families are living in homes where, night after night, noise from selfish and inconsiderate neighbours makes it difficult for them and their children to sleep. Existing powers to tackle daytime noise are effective and approximately 80% of local authorities already have some out of hours noise service. But the powers to tackle noise at night can be insufficient and slow to implement.

3.6   As a start, we will make it easier to use existing powers so that people making excessive noise at night can be given a warning and 10 minutes to stop. If they do not, local authorities will be able to issue a £100 FPN. If the fixed penalty is not paid or not effective then further and tougher action will be taken such as removal of the TV or stereo used to make the noise. Communities should not have to tolerate noise nuisance in any form of housing. If necessary, further enforcement action should be taken such as injunctions, evictions from tenancies or ASBO's to ensure this menace is dealt with.

3.7   In addition, it is important to be able to tackle excessive noise from pubs, clubs and other entertainment venues. At the moment environmental health officers can require an establishment to take specific immediate action to stop the source of the noise but they cannot require immediate closure of the premises. We will give environmental health officers the power to shut down, with immediate effect, any establishments that cause public nuisance by the noise they create, where closure is necessary to stop this.

3.8   Environmental health officers have a key part to play in the management, protection and enhancement of our public environments. In particular, they possess the relevant training, experience and technical skills to assess whether a noise or nuisance is 'actionable' under the appropriate legislation. Consequently where anti-social behaviour involves a noise or nuisance element, environmental health professionals are likely to have a pivotal role in its successful resolution.

Leeds City Council Noise Team

Leeds City Council introduced an out-of-hours noise service in 2001, offering a noise complaint phoneline, supported by a dedicated team of environmental health professionals.

In the first year of operation, the number of domestic noise complaints doubled. As a result of more information from residents and having an out-of-hours team, there been a 412 per cent increase in enforcement action. The service has led to a 57% in noise incidents that are dealt with by the police. This has freed up 1,940 hours of police time.

Fireworks

3.9 Most people enjoy the use of fireworks on Bonfire Night or on other special occasions during the year. However the use of fireworks outside the traditional season, sometimes late at night is becoming more commonplace, with the resulting increase in noise and nuisance. There are some people that have taken to using them not only to cause distress or nuisance but in extreme cases as weapons to cause criminal damage or injury. Action must be taken to prevent further misery to more people and their pet's lives and to protect their property.

3.10 Legislation already exists covering the criminal misuse of fireworks. In October 2002, the DTI launched a campaign to encourage local councils to use the existing powers. The fireworks industry is also playing a major part. They introduced a voluntary ban on 'airbombs' from 1 January 2003. These cheap noisy fireworks contribute significantly to the problem being responsible for an estimated 30 million explosions a year.

3.11 We are also aware that many of those responsible for the irresponsible use of fireworks are under 18 and it is at present illegal to sell fireworks to those under 18. However, further action is needed and we are wholeheartedly behind the changes going through Parliament in a Private Member's Bill that will review all the rules and regulations governing fireworks and introduce a more effective regime.

'Crack Houses'

3.12 For sometime local authorities, the police and local communities have been frustrated by their lack of powers to close down premises – rented, owner occupied or otherwise – where Class A drugs are being sold and used. We are determined to ensure that the ruin they can cause in communities is stopped.

3.13 We have to close down these properties from which drug dealers operate, or new dealers will simply move in. These dealers are sophisticated and devious in their methods. They can prey on vulnerable people compelling them to give over their property whilst they deal and use drugs, and intimidate both the residents and neighbours, sometimes making them too frightened to speak out for fear of retribution.

3.14   The new powers will give police the power, after consulting the local authority, to issue notice of impending closure, ratified by a court, which will enable the property to be closed within 48 hours and sealed for a fixed period of up to six months. Drug dealers will be dealt with through the courts and the property will be recovered by the landlord.

Airguns and replica weapons

3.15   In 2001/2002, there were 12,340 recorded offences where air weapons were used, of which 166 involved serious injuries, and in two cases the injuries proved fatal.

3.16   Some people use airguns to break windows, hurt pets and even shoot at people. This conduct is wholly unacceptable and we are determined to deal with it. For this reason, we have decided to increase the age at which young people can own an air weapon from 14 to 17 and to tighten up on when they can be used without adult supervision. In addition, we will introduce a new arrestable offence of having an air weapon in a public place without lawful authority or reasonable excuse.

3.17   The misuse of replica firearms has also resulted in considerable alarm. In inner city areas the police estimate that 50% of call-outs of armed police result from the sighting of an imitation firearm. There is a real risk that the person carrying the imitation will be shot if they appear to threaten the police or members of the public. There is also evidence that replica firearms are used to threaten victims and that some young people, particularly in inner city areas, have taken to carrying replica firearms as fashion accessories and to intimidate others.

3.18   This cannot be ignored and we intend to combat it by introducing a new offence of having an imitation firearm in a public place without lawful authority or reasonable excuse. As with air weapons, this offence will have a power to arrest and to seize attached to it.

3.19   A problem has emerged in recent years in relation to certain air weapons that are powered by self-contained air cartridge systems. These weapons have proved to be vulnerable to conversion in a variety of relatively straightforward ways to take conventional ammunition. Because of this and their very realistic appearance they have become popular with certain criminals and have been used in a number of serious crimes including seven homicides. No viable way has been found of making these weapons less easily convertible. We intend, therefore, to ban the importation, sale and manufacture of these weapons. Current owners will be allowed to keep their guns, but will require a licence. Those people not wishing to obtain a licence will be given an opportunity to hand them in to the police.

3.20   These new changes are part of the Government's overall strategy to tackle gun crime. In January this year, we announced a major tightening up of gun laws including plans for a 5-year minimum sentence for illegal possession and use of a firearm.

Graffiti and Litter

3.21   In October 2002 the Government published *Living Places Powers, Rights, Responsibilities* a major consultative document which set out twenty-seven options for reforming legislation relating to public space. In taking forward our agenda on anti-social behaviour we will be informed by the responses to this consultation. However, there are a number of areas that can be improved immediately to the benefit of all the community.

3.22   Real reductions in the amount of graffiti can be made if spray paints were made harder to obtain for those most likely to abuse them. We will create a new power to make it an offence to sell spray paints to young people aged under 18 years. We will also, through the Criminal Justice Bill, give the police new powers to enable them to search for items which they suspect may be intended for use in causing criminal damage, such as spray paints.

3.23   In some communities, graffiti, vandalism and rubbish are dealt with promptly. Elsewhere it takes months. An example where local authorities have made a significant difference is with the clean up of graffiti. Some local authorities have set up 'Hot lines' where members of the public can report graffiti which they have spotted. Street and community wardens will report and in some cases also remove graffiti. Many aim for a target of removing racist and offensive graffiti within 24 hours. Private companies and businesses also have a key role in tackling graffiti and other environmental problems quickly and effectively.

3.24   Graffiti is often committed by organised groups. It has become a highly organised industry and the police are targeting the offenders by identifying the many unique 'tags' which gangs and individuals use to mark out their territory. The British Transport Police are involved in intelligence and surveillance work to apprehend graffiti gangs who target trains in depots and railway infrastructure. CCTV and graffiti-proof paints deter casual graffiti perpetrators but intensive surveillance particularly at night is required by the police to tackle persistent organised gangs.

3.25   We are introducing legislation to address the issue of rubbish ridden areas by, extending the strategic powers of local authorities to include not only litter but also other aspects of environmental quality such as vandalism or fly-posting. We will also extend local authorities intervention powers so that they can clean all types of relevant land, and then claim their costs from the owner of that land.

> **London Borough of Barnet – Graffiti clean up operation**
>
> Barnet police, working with the local authority, have successfully prosecuted 20 graffiti perpetrators operating in the area in the early months of 2002. Trained 'town keepers' have been recruited to patrol zones in town centres, dealing with litter, graffiti, fly posting and fly tipping. They have access to digital cameras to photograph graffiti for police intelligence. The scheme has been successful in securing community involvement by signing up shopkeepers and street traders to facilitate the clean-up of shutters in the daytime.

3.26   Local authorities already have powers to fine people for littering and dog fouling. Under the Local Government Bill currently before Parliament they will now be able to keep the proceeds of FPN's that they impose. DEFRA are currently considering whether local authorities should also be able to retain some of the proceeds towards the cost of enforcement for all FPN's related to environmental offences.

Fly-tipping

3.27   Some people do not properly dispose of their waste – they dump it in the street, in their neighbour's gardens, in alleyways and in parks. Fly-tipping – illegal disposal of waste – seriously reduces the quality of the local environment. Current legislation includes powers that are available to the Environment Agency for tackling fly-tipping. Few of the powers are available to local authorities and the current division of responsibilities between the Environment Agency and local authorities is subject to a voluntary agreement, which is often unclear.

3.28   The current system will be re-balanced so that local authorities are responsible for dealing with local fly-tipping incidents. We will give local authorities powers to investigate fly-tipping and to stop, search and seize vehicles being used for this purpose so that they can deal with small scale fly-tipping. We will also be issuing statutory guidance that will help to reinforce the new approach we are taking towards dealing with fly-tipping and to help clarify respective responsibilities.

Abandoned vehicles

3.29   It is estimated that some 238,000 cars were abandoned in the year 2000 alone. Their management is a heavy and increasing burden on Local Authorities, police and – due to their tendency to attract arson – fire services. Much has been done to improve this situation:

- the period of notice for the removal of an abandoned car has been reduced to 24 hours from 7 days;
- £2.7 million is being invested by Government to link the Driver and Vehicle Licensing Agency (DVLA) and local councils which will make it easier and quicker to trace and clarify the ownership of abandoned vehicles;
- we have given Community Support Officers and accredited persons powers to remove an abandoned vehicle immediately, where it is in a dangerous position, causing an obstruction or contravening a parking regulation;
- the Government is also reviewing vehicle registration and licensing, to reduce evasion and to bear down on vehicle crime. The 2002 Finance Act contained provisions under which the responsibility for licensing and taxing vehicles will be placed on the registered keeper, who will remain liable for doing so until such time that the DVLA has properly been notified of a change of keeper.

3.30   The DVLA is responsible for enforcement action against untaxed vehicles and the majority of abandoned vehicles are untaxed. They are working closely with other enforcement organisations in schemes to target both unlicensed and abandoned vehicles. It has also initiated a number of schemes in which local authorities have been given DVLA powers to clamp and remove untaxed vehicles – in particular in Newham, Hastings, Wandsworth and Croydon.

Tyne and Wear Task Force

This multi agency task force was established in the West end of Newcastle. It identifies owners as rapidly as possible and removes the vehicle to a Council car compound. The location of vehicle fires are plotted using a database that identifies trends and this then informs the police and fire Services' response. This has cut down arson incidents.

Tackling intimidating and offensive behaviour

Drunken 'yob' culture

3.31   The growth of the 24-hour city culture brings many positive benefits; more vibrant town centres, more income and jobs for the local economy and more leisure opportunities and choice for individuals. The great majority of those out at night are there for fun and have no intention of committing any crime. However, a minority will end up behaving anti-socially, urinating in the streets, fighting, intimidating bystanders and passers-by and causing criminal damage. Those getting drunk at least weekly are five times more likely than their peers to be involved in fighting or violent crime.

3.32   There is evidence that flexible licensing hours lead to less binge drinking and that staggered closing times significantly reduce 'peak' disturbance and disorder and prevent the need to disperse large numbers of people.

3.33   The Licensing Bill, currently before Parliament, introduces a new licensing scheme that is currently scheduled to come into force in 2004. The Bill contains a number of measures to tackle crime, disorder and anti-social behaviour. These include:

- Expanding existing court powers, on application by the police, to close all licensed premises within a specified geographical area for up to 24 hours where disorder is occurring or anticipated.
- Expanding existing police powers introduced in December 2001 to close down disorderly and excessively noisy pubs, nightclubs, restaurants and hotels instantly for up to 24 hours. Permanent or temporary measures may be imposed on a premises licence following these closures by the court or by a licensing authority following a review.
- A new offence of selling alcohol to children anywhere, not just at licensed premises, will be introduced. It will also reproduce the offences of buying alcohol on behalf of a person under 18, and of knowingly permitting a sale to an under 18.
- Police and local residents, among others, will be able to call for a review of any premises licence at any time. A review could lead to a range of measures including revocation, suspension or modification of the conditions of the licence (e.g. by requiring additional security or CCTV to be provided).
- Amending existing legislation by extending police powers to confiscate alcohol in designated public places to include sealed containers and enable the police to seek court orders banning the sale of alcohol on train routes (either temporarily or permanently).

3.34   These measures will complement existing police powers to tackle under-age drinking. It is, for example, an offence to sell alcohol to under 18s on licensed premises and police can confiscate alcohol from under-age drinkers in public places. We will work with the police to ensure these measures are effectively enforced.

3.35   The statutory guidance for licensing authorities that will accompany the Bill will include model conditions that could be attached to premises licences, in appropriate circumstances, for the promotion of the licensing objectives introduced by the Bill, for instance to address issues of crime and disorder. These could, for example, include the installation of CCTV, participation in a radio pager scheme or the use of toughened drinking glasses. The guidance will also make clear that an application for a new licensed premise could be turned down on the basis that the build up of licensed premises was leading to problems. This would need to be evidenced by the police.

3.36   Consultation on the Government's National Alcohol Harm Reduction Strategy has just ended. It included questions on links between alcohol and anti-social behaviour. We will consider the results of this exercise in taking forward our strategy on anti-social behaviour. The strategy, due to be published this summer, will bring forward further measures to tackle alcohol-related crime and disorder.

City Centre Safe

City Centre Safe was introduced two years ago in Manchester city centre to reduce alcohol related crime. It is a partnership across the city, local business, universities and the drinks industry. The scheme introduced:

- by-laws allowing police officers to seize, and dispose of bottles, glasses and cans from people who are found drinking in public in the city centre;
- late night bus transport from the city to outlying areas of Manchester until 03.30 am on Friday and Saturday nights. Bus stops are jointly patrolled by police and bus company staff who act as loaders, filtering out the drunk and aggressive passengers;
- the 'Peter Street Initiative' where bars and pubs in the Peter Street area joined together to pay for one police officer on Friday and Saturday nights; and
- a 'Nite Net' radio system allowing pubs, clubs, CCTV and police officers to have a direct line of communication during the hours of darkness.

Over two years the scheme has achieved a 17% reduction in serious assaults.

3.37   Urinating against the walls of people's shops, houses and offices is unacceptable in a civilised society. Local by-laws are often used to deal with this problem and those caught are sometimes charged with being drunk and disorderly. The Criminal Justice and Police Act 2001 introduced a scheme for issuing FPN's for disorder of this type. Police forces piloting this scheme have found FPNs an effective way of tackling this behaviour.

Street drinking

3.38   Street drinkers can take over public spaces such as playgrounds and parks. Many local authorities across the country have introduced designated areas, where the consumption of alcohol on the streets is not allowed and we strongly support this action. The police and

Community Support Officers, as well as others are used to enforce the by-laws and will in the future enforce FPNs.

3.39   Many areas are interested in establishing 'wet centres' for people who might otherwise drink in town centres and intimidate members of the public. Existing services – such as the Handel Day Centre in Nottingham and the Anchor Centre in Leicester – provide a range of services for their clients and ensure that people are able to drink in a supportive environment without intimidating members of the public or the local community. The Homelessness Directorate in the Office of the Deputy Prime Minister and the King's Fund are planning a research project into the impact and effectiveness of wet centres. This will look to review the work of wet centres with their clients and to highlight good practice in the establishment and running of a centre.

Begging

3.40   No one in this country should beg – it is degrading for them, embarrassing for those they approach and often a detriment to the very areas where environmental and social improvements are crucial to the broader regeneration of the community itself. We need to tackle the nuisance and intimidation caused to those going about their lawful business, by people who persistently beg.

3.41   There are places for rough sleepers to sleep at night, there is support and treatment available for their health needs and drug habits, and there are benefits available to pay for food and rent. The reality is that the majority of people who beg are doing so to sustain a drug habit, and are often caught up in much more serious crime. When members of the public give them money on the street it does not help them deal with their problems.

3.42   The public can feel intimidated by people begging at cash points, outside shops or asking them for money in the street or on trains. Using children and pets to make money from begging is completely unacceptable. Measures to tackle begging are a move to reduce levels of anti-social behaviour, to protect more vulnerable people from being drawn into street activity and to guard against the sustaining of harmful drug addictions.

3.43   The Government is addressing the underlying causes and tackling its persistent nature. The current offence of begging will be made recordable under the National Police Records (Recordable Offences) Regulations 2000. This will make begging convictions a part of an individual's criminal record and enable police forces to fingerprint offenders. This will not only lead to more appropriate sentencing but also will enable the police to keep track of persistent offenders.

3.44   Appropriate sentencing needs to take account of the reasons why some people beg. The Criminal Justice Bill will provide sentencers with a new power which will enable them to deal more effectively with persistent beggars. After three or more convictions, the Court will be able to impose a community sentence, including drug treatment.

> **Bristol City Council Street Wise Project**
>
> In Bristol begging was escalating out of control. The local authority, in partnership with the police, drug action team, voluntary sector and business community decided to run a 'Street Wise' campaign to tackle begging in the city centre. This found that:
> – 100% of beggars have a dependency on Class A drugs.
> – 95% had a previous conviction for robbery or violent crime.
> The 'Street Wise' project in the last 6 months has made over 300 arrests. Many people, who had previously refused drug services, are now in treatment. The project has meant a visible reduction in begging in the City.

Kerb crawling and prostitution

3.45   Prostitution can cause distress and nuisance to local residents. Resulting problems include discarded condoms and needles, traffic problems caused by kerb crawlers and telephone boxes defaced by cards advertising sexual services. In 2001 the police were given new powers of arrest for the offence of kerb crawling and a new offence was established to deal with the placing of prostitute's cards in telephone boxes. We also need to offer support to prostitutes who are vulnerable themselves – who may for example be underage or addicted to drugs. The Sexual Offences Bill, currently before Parliament offers more protection to those at risk by introducing new offences to deal with sexual exploitation. In particular paying for sex with a child and causing, inciting, controlling or arranging child prostitution will carry heavy maximum prison sentences.

3.46   Those convicted of kerb crawling receive a fine up to £1,000. As part of the changes in the Criminal Justice Bill 'Conditional Cautions' will be introduced that makes it a condition that offenders are forced to face up to the consequences of their behaviour.

3.47   As an additional deterrent, courts will be able to take away the driving licenses of those convicted of kerb crawling. Courts will be notified of provisions under Powers of Criminal Courts (Sentencing) Act 2000 that enable them to consider disqualifying from driving anyone convicted of relevant offences, as an additional penalty. Disqualification can last for as long as the court considers appropriate.

Off road biking

3.48   To help combat misuse of off-road motor vehicles we will remind the courts that they have the power to disqualify and remove people's driving licences. This is to tackle the misuse of bikes in parts of the countryside used by walkers and complements the powers to seize vehicles being used anti-socially, in the Police Reform Act 2002.

CHAPTER 3 SUMMARY OF NEW MEASURES

Enforcing local standards and tackling the abuse of our environment

- Streamline existing powers for local authorities to enable them to issue fixed penalty notices to people making excessive noise at night.
- Environmental health officers will have the power to shut down establishments that persistently create noise nuisance, with immediate effect.
- Wholehearted Government support will be given to a Private Members Bill that will review all regulations governing fireworks and introduce a more effective regime.
- New powers will be given to the police to issue notice of impending closure on a property where Class A drugs are being sold and used.
- The age at which young people can own an air weapon will be increased from 14 to 17.
- New arrestable offences of having an air weapon or imitation firearm in a public place without lawful authority or reasonable excuse will be introduced.
- The Government will ban the importation, sale and manufacture of air weapons that can be easily converted to take conventional ammunition.
- We will create a new offence of selling spray paints to young people aged under 18 and, under the Criminal Justice Bill, police will be given new powers to search for items that they suspect may be intended for causing criminal damage.
- Local authorities will be given extended strategic powers to tackle all aspects of environmental quality. We will also extend local authorities' intervention powers so that they can clean all types of relevant land, and then claim their costs from the owner of that land.
- Local authorities will be able to keep the proceeds of any fixed penalty notices for littering and dog fouling under the Local Government Bill.
- Local authorities will be given new powers to tackle fly-tipping
- The Government is reviewing vehicle registration and licensing, to reduce evasion and bear down on vehicle crime.

Tackling intimidating and offensive behaviour

- The Licensing Bill will introduce a number of measures to address the anti-social behaviour associated with drinking, both in licensed premises and public places.
- The Licensing Bill will also introduce the ability for licensing authorities to reject an application for a new licensed premise on the basis that a build up of licensed premises was leading to problems.
- Local authorities will be encouraged to introduce designated areas where the consumption of alcohol will not be allowed.
- The current offence of begging will be made recordable.
- The Sexual Offences Bill introduces heavy maximum prison sentences for paying for sex with a child and causing, inciting, controlling or arranging child prostitution. The Criminal Justice Bill introduces new conditional cautions for kerb-crawlers. Courts will also be notified of provisions that enable them to consider disqualifying from driving anyone convicted of kerb crawling.
- Courts will be notified of similar powers to disqualify those driving off-road without authority.

Chapter Four

LOCAL PROBLEM, LOCAL ACTION

4.1   The Government will support local communities in tackling anti-social behaviour. By ensuring that the necessary powers are available to the police and other enforcement agencies; through the resources that we provide to the police, local authorities, probation and other public services; and by supporting the spread of best practice in tackling the problem. However anti-social behaviour is a problem experienced at local level and therefore requires effective action locally. This includes individuals, families, residents associations, community groups and also the public services. It is vital that the right people have the power, the authority and the support to tackle anti-social behaviour.

4.2   Effective local action requires:

- clear local leadership, through local Crime and Disorder Reduction Partnerships, to identify the local anti-social behaviour problems and to ensure that all the local agencies work together to deal with them
- clear local standards on the types anti-social behaviour that will not be tolerated that are developed and shared with local people and communities, enforced by local agencies especially the police, and upheld by the criminal justice system
- support from local people, who are prepared to come forward with information, willing to challenge unacceptable behaviour, and committed to dealing with local problems, knowing that they will be supported by their neighbours, friends and professional agencies
- an understanding that local councils, housing associations, the police and other local agencies must be accountable to local people for the way in which they tackle anti-social behaviour

Crime and Disorder Reduction Partnerships

4.3   Crime and Disorder Reduction Partnerships (CDRPs) must take they local lead in tackling anti-social behaviour. CDRPs were established in 1998 to assess crime and disorder in their area and develop and implement strategies to reduce them. They bring together local authorities, the police and other local stakeholders to co-ordinate action locally. As such they have a crucial role in enabling and encouraging communities to address anti-social behaviour.

4.4 We will ensure that the strategies CDRPs produce now also set out action to tackle anti-social behaviour across the local area. CDRPs will audit the extent of local problems, actively consult with their local community and take forward a strategy to tackle the problem.

4.5 It is essential that all agencies acting in this area play their part in implementing this strategy. An important lever to ensure this happens is Section 17 of the Crime and Disorder Act 1998. This places a duty on local authorities and others 'to exercise their functions with due regard to the likely effect of the exercise of those functions on, and do all that they reasonably can to prevent crime and disorder, in their areas'. This, together with the duty on CDRPs to publish within their strategies action for dealing with anti-social behaviour, means that not only will local strategies have to set out how anti-social behaviour will be tackled, but delivery of those strategies will have to be mainstreamed in the delivery of local services.

4.6 In order to tackle anti-social behaviour effectively, it is important that local agencies share and exchange relevant information. Each relevant authority should disclose relevant information, including personal information, to other relevant authorities in a way that is consistent with legal requirements. In some areas, the exchange of information is governed by an information exchange protocol. This protocol ensures that all parties are sharing information in ways that are consistent with legal requirements, but also meet the needs of the partnership to tackle anti-social behaviour.

4.7 It is also vital that CDRP strategies are properly communicated to local people so that everyone is aware of the local services in place to tackle anti-social behaviour and knows how to access them.

4.8 Nothing undermines public confidence more than the sense that no one is taking anti-social behaviour seriously. To be told by the police that it is not their priority, by the housing department that you should contact the police, by the youth service that it's not their job, leaves victims of anti-social behaviour feeling isolated and unsupported.

4.9 As local anti-social behaviour strategies are developed a great deal of effort needs to go into the way in which they are communicated to the public. Most people will accept that they cannot always have a police response every time a young person is a nuisance – as long as they are told what is being done to identify the perpetrators, how they can help, and what action will be taken. Whichever agency they contact for help, they need to be given a consistent response, not sent from one place to another. It is also vital that when an ASBO is issued, the public are informed.

4.10   CDRPs will need to involve a number of partners in the development and implementation of action to tackle anti-social behaviour. All the key departments within the local authority will be important such as housing, social services, education and the youth service. The police, the fire service as well local primary health care trusts and the drug action teams are all needed to make the long-term difference in communities.

4.11   Once the strategies are in place it is vital that the culture is one where enforcement is at the centre. Without the police taking action to track down perpetrators, without the local authority taking a tough stance on the eviction of tenants for anti-social behaviour, without the environmental health officers dealing with noise nuisance then the strategies are meaningless and the community loses faith. The enforcement of these strategies is the critical element.

4.12   It is important that communities are not afraid to use parks, playgrounds, streets and shopping centres. Young people gathering together in groups can be very intimidating to the public and trouble does sometimes occur when gangs gather together in the street. In the year 2000, 32% of respondents to the BCS cited teenagers hanging around in the street as a big problem in their area.

4.13   The police, in consultation with local authorities, will therefore be given the ability to designate areas with significant levels of anti-social behaviour. Within these specified areas the police will be able to disperse groups of people and will have access to automatic, fast-track child curfew powers.

Police

4.14   The publication of the White Paper 'Policing a New Century: A Blueprint for Reform' in December 2001, launched a radical programme of reform for the police service. Legislation followed with the Police Reform Act 2002 and, in November 2002, the first National Policing Plan was published, making tackling anti-social behaviour a key priority for the first time. This sets out the Home Secretary's strategic priorities for the police service for the next three years. Key amongst these was working with partners to tackle anti-social behaviour and disorder.

4.15   The National Policing Plan sets out what the police are expected to achieve to make our communities safer and how their performance will be measured. Each police force and authority is expected to use the National Policing Plan as a framework for their local planning and to take account of it in their local strategic three-year plans that will describe how the national strategic priorities will be translated into action on the ground.

4.16 Some three-year plans have already been submitted to the Home Secretary setting out how they will tackle anti-social behaviour. One force has undertaken to recruit 60 Community Support Officers who will be deployed along with special constables to deal with anti-social behaviour. Another has established an anti-social behaviour unit to co-ordinate work and has local objectives of reducing anti-social behaviour by using ABCs and ASBOs.

4.17 The National Intelligence Model (NIM) brings together good practice to form a standardised model for the management of intelligence. The National Policing Plan requires police forces to apply the NIM. Some forces are already using it to help combat anti-social behaviour but all forces should apply it to inform and support their strategy to address anti-social behaviour, which the National Policing Plan requires them to draw up and implement. The importance of the NIM is that it enables the police to understand where the crime and disorder problems lie, and develop appropriate tactics in response. This should include, for example, how best to use their resources, including the extended police family of Community Support Officers and members of accredited community safety schemes. It will also help the police determine with the local authority whether in certain areas they need to use the new powers to designate areas to disperse groups and use the child curfew powers.

4.18 The Government is increasing the capacity of police officers and the 'extended police family' to tackle anti-social behaviour. This includes:

- Funding more police officers. We are on track to achieve the target of 132,500 to be reached by 2004.
- By the end of March this year 1,200 Community Support Officers in twenty-seven police force areas will be patrolling in our neighbourhoods and communities. We are on track to deliver 4,000 Community Support Officers by the end of 2005.

4.19 The police's role in tackling anti-social behaviour is critical. Without their wholehearted support, energy and commitment, it is impossible for any community to tackle the behaviour of the very people that ruin their lives. Enforcement action – ASBOs or criminal proceedings – will create the backbone needed to shift the culture of resignation to some of these problems. We are asking police forces around the country to give priority to tackling anti social behaviour.

> **Kent Police**
>
> Kent police use a multi-agency approach called 'Joint Family Management' to tackle anti-social behaviour. They have produced a Problem Family Manual which details a four stage approach from support to sanction depending on how entrenched the difficulties are and how the family respond to previous interventions.
> - Practitioners sharing information on family (within guidelines), visit by authorities/letter of warning
> - Acceptable Behaviour Contracts, extra support for parents (including mental health), school consultation for additional support needs etc
> - Technical surveillance, joint action warrants/TV licence/Benefits/Environmental health, Child Safety Order, YOT referral, Child Protection, relocation
> - Injunctions, evictions, ASBO, Parenting Order, Care Order Prosecution

Special Constabulary

4.20   The Special Constabulary has long assisted regular police officers to police and reassure communities. As such their role in helping to tackle anti-social behaviour is crucial.

4.21   The Home Office is presently working with ten police forces under the Specials Champions Initiative to help develop good practice in every aspect of the work of Specials. Later this year we will draw on this work to launch our new vision for Specials, aiming to increase substantially the number and effectiveness and to underline the essential their role they can play in reassuring the public, tackling crime with regular officers, and dealing with anti-social behaviour.

> **Specials**
>
> **The Bridgend Division of South Wales Police** were awarded the Team Award at the Ferrers 'National Special of the Year' ceremony 2002 for their work in the Pencoed Community in South Wales. The team of Specials worked together to provide a sustained focus on identified local targets and 'hotspots' where vandalism and verbally threatening and abusive behaviour was making life generally miserable for the local community. The award recognised the team's success in achieving a decrease in crime, after-school detention and exclusion figures. The team's consistent presence in Pencoed for 6 months clearly made a real difference to people's lives and the Special Constabulary received many letters of thanks.
>
> Since the awards ceremony, similar schemes have concentrated on the more socially deprived area of the Bridgend division, resulting in a reduction in 'youth annoyance'. The Specials have also focussed on the diversion of young people from the brink of criminality to more empowering schemes that are run in partnership with South Wales Police and Youth Community Education. The team's work has brought a heightened sense of reassurance within the locality, allowing the streets of Bridgend to be reclaimed by the community and helping to regenerate community spirit in the area.

Accreditation Schemes

4.22   The Police Reform Act 2002 allowed the creation of community safety accreditation schemes. Accreditation schemes will allow more people to exercise enforcement powers, including FPNs, with the agreement of Chief Constables.

4.23   At the moment, a wide range of agencies, from the public, private and voluntary sectors are involved in vitally important community safety work in support of the police. This includes street crime wardens and members of the private security industry who work in shopping centres and sports grounds. The Police Reform Act allows Chief Constables to accredit these individuals in order to demonstrate to the public that they meet certain standards relating to training and good character and have close links to the police in terms of communication and sharing of intelligence, including use of the National Intelligence Model.

4.24   The Police Reform Act 2002 allowed accredited community safety officers to be given powers to deal with major public nuisances such as dog fouling, litter, cycling on the pavement and confiscation of alcohol and tobacco from those who are underaged. We will use the Anti-Social Behaviour Bill to extend these powers so that accredited people are able to issue FPNs for disorder offences, in line with the powers already given to the police and Community Support Officers.

4.25   There is currently considerable interest in accreditation schemes, the first of which, we hope will come into force on 1 April this year. But in order to support the development of accreditation schemes, the Home Office is working with the Association of Chief Police Officers, and other agencies, on guidance for those wishing to set up and take part in accreditation schemes

4.26   The introduction of Community Support Officers and Community Safety Accreditation Schemes has given the police, local authorities and other agencies a range of additional options for tackling anti-social behaviour and minor disorder. To make best use of these options, local agencies need to be clear about the respective roles and responsibilities of community support officers, neighbourhood wardens and other community safety professionals and how they might most effectively work together. The Office of the Deputy Prime Minister and the Home Office are producing guidance this year.

Local authorities

4.27   The role of local government in tacking anti-social behaviour is of equal importance to that of the police. Together they are the twin elements of ensuring that rules are set and enforced locally. Everyone else can play their part but the role of the police and local authorities is essential in delivery of action.

4.28   Local authorities are absolutely vital in tackling anti-social behaviour. They are accountable to the local community and they are best placed to respond to its needs. They will lead the drive to tackle this problem with the support of key local partners and central Government.

4.29   Much of the drive to take anti-social behaviour has come from residents and tenants in council property. In turn, staff in local authority housing departments have been at the forefront of developing new approaches and strategies. We are indebted to many of those people for fearlessly pioneering new ways to tackle the problem and to make the link across their work to crime and disorder.

4.30   Much of the good practice highlighted in this document is based on their work and that of local police officers who have on behalf of the community taken a stand against anti-social behaviour.

4.31   Local authorities have many of the levers in place to tackle the problem; from providing support to young people at risk to taking action to evict an anti-social tenant. They need the police, the courts and many others to work in partnership.

4.32   There are countless examples around the country of local authorities taking steps to tackle anti-social behaviour. This good practice needs to be reinforced, built upon and promulgated. Just a few examples are highlighted in the box below.

> **Environmental Health Officers in Doncaster**
>
> Environmental Health Officers in Doncaster's noise team use innovative face-to-face methods to confront offenders with the impact of their behaviour. For instance, they play back digital recordings of the noise they have made and ask the perpetrator if they would tolerate it. This happens before more formal action is tried. They report this has led to a decline in these problems.

Neighbourhood Nuisance in Manchester

Manchester City Council's Neighbourhood Nuisance Team takes action against perpetrators of anti-social behaviour and supports residents who give evidence. The team tackle nuisance vigorously – using Housing Act injunctions and Anti-Social Behaviour Orders. It was one of the first in the country and pioneered new ways of working including the use of leaflets that outline the action taken against those on orders to ensure the community knew what they had achieved

Community Safety in Leeds

Leeds City Council has set up a 40 person Anti-social Behaviour Unit that tackles anti-social behaviour across the city and across all forms of tenure. It works in partnership with its own legal team and local police. In February 2003 they set up a anti social behaviour phone-line for anyone in Leeds to report anti-social behaviour.

Liverpool Anti-Social Behaviour Unit (LASBU)

LASBU has developed a Safer Neighbourhoods Service (SNS) to provide a 'One Stop' anti-social behaviour prevention service. The Safer Neighbourhoods Service provides a range of services, including:

- the co-ordination of activities and action planning in 'hot spot' areas of the city;
- a legal service dealing with Anti-Social Behaviour Orders, Injunctions, Parenting Orders and other measures;
- area-based Enforcement Teams, trained in the use of surveillance to identify the perpetrators of anti-social behaviour;
- a Prevention Team, working with local schools and police to provide training for teaching staff, a referral system for pupils at risk, Acceptable Behaviour Contracts and parenting courses.

4.33   Social services also have a critical role to play, not least through meeting their responsibilities under Section 17 of the Crime and Disorder Act. There are good examples of social services, education and housing departments working together in Crime and Disorder Partnerships. The more we do to ensure preventative action is taken to help families or individuals in crisis the more effective that is both for those clients but also for the community more widely. Social services also have to play their part in enforcement, in assisting to maintain the standards of behaviour required across the community.

4.34   The youth service is also a key player in a local authority's drive against anti-social behaviour. A comprehensive programme of work is underway to improve Youth Service provision. In December, the Government published *Transforming Youth Work – Resourcing Excellent Youth Service*, which set out what Government expects of high quality youth services. It sets clear targets and emphasises the need for Youth Services to work with young people who are most at risk of committing anti-social behaviour.

4.35   Other parts of Local Government also have an important role. Safety and security must be key considerations in the design and planning of our local environment in order to 'design out' crime as much as possible. For instance, in South Yorkshire bus shelters have been re-designed to make them safer places to be and less of a target for vandalism. Improved street lighting also helps reduce crime and anti-social behaviour – especially if accompanied by other environmental improvements. It deters the criminal and reassures the potential victim. It can also reassure the public that an area is improving, leading to increased confidence, cohesion and social control within an area.

Tackling anti-social behaviour in housing

4.36 A key role for local authorities is that of landlord. As with everything in tackling anti-social behaviour, it is vital that perpetrators understand that keeping their home is dependent on their behaviour not ruining whole communities. Intimidating neighbours, harassing families in the street, dumping rubbish on doorsteps or allowing children to get out of control is unacceptable. We intend to take action to make the perpetrators deal with their behaviour or they will be evicted themselves. Proper contractual agreements should be in place as with good social or private sector landlords, which make it the norm whatever the tenure, for landlords and tenants to behave in a civilised fashion.

4.37 Currently local authorities have strong powers to deal with anti-social behaviour, and often use them effectively. They can take action against their own tenants and can also protect their tenants against problems caused by others.

4.38 To build on and strengthen this work, we are proposing that all social landlords should publish their policies and procedures on anti-social behaviour. Tenants should know the tools their landlords have at their disposal, and how their complaints will be dealt with.

4.39 We also want to ensure that all social housing providers – local housing authorities, housing action trusts, charitable housing trusts and registered social landlords – have the a range of powers to enable them to take action against anti-social tenants. We will introduce the following measures:

- *Extend the scope of injunctions and make them available to other social landlords*

All social landlords will be able to obtain county court injunctions to exclude perpetrators of anti-social behaviour very quickly from a specified area, including if necessary their own home. Changes to injunctions will make it easier to exclude perpetrators from the areas where they have been causing trouble, including if necessary their own home; will widen the range of people who can be protected to include staff and contractors of the landlord; will widen the circumstances in which perpetrators can be arrested for breaching an injunction – e.g. to include hate behaviour and will bring powers of registered social landlords RSLs more in line with those of local housing authorities. Social landlords will be able to take action to protect their tenants, as well as take action against them.

Housing Action Trusts (HATs) improve social housing in local communities and undertake a wide range of community activities. They are landlords for roughly 25,000 residents in about 12,000 households. To protect their residents from anti-social behaviour, or tackle such behaviour amongst residents, by using an anti-social behaviour order HATs have to rely on the police or local authority to act for them. We want to enable HATs to apply directly for ASBOs so that they have greater scope to tackle anti-social behaviour. This will bring them into line with other social housing providers.

- *Loss of security for anti-social tenants*

Anti-social tenants will lose their secure or assured tenancies and lose their security of tenure through 'demoted tenancies' until their behaviour is addressed. They will lose the 'right to buy' and eviction will be easier if no improvement is made. If they do not reform their behaviour, eviction from these probationary tenancies is easier than from secure or assured tenancies. If their behaviour improves, they can regain their secure or assured tenancy status, 'right to buy' and associated rights.

Social landlords will also be able to extend the initial 12-month period of the introductory, starter, or probationary tenancy, by a further period of 6 months if they have continuing concerns about behaviour.

- *Ensuring the needs of the community are fully taken into account*

When possession cases go to court, judges will now consider the impact of the anti-social behaviour on the victim, witnesses and the wider community.

- *Improve partnership working*

Although we have to ensure that swift and effective action can be taken against anti-social tenants, it is vital that where possible the behaviour is tackled, the tenancy saved and the family is not moved. Constant forced moves not only damage family life, they also create unstable communities. There is a range of measures that every area can put in place to prevent anti-social behaviour and ensuring disruption is minimised.

4.40   In many areas, the relationship between housing and social services is effective and 'early warning' mechanisms are in place so that, where there is the threat of eviction support and supervision is provided to the family and children which can sometimes reduce the problem.

Portsmouth City Council and Hampshire Constabulary each have a named ASB contact officer (the Crime and Disorder Officer and the Operational Chief Inspector respectively). All Registered Social Landlords in Portsmouth will have a named ASB Contact Officer by 1 April 2003. Their role is to liaise on anti social behaviour cases requiring an inter agency response. Portsmouth City Council's Crime and Disorder Unit oversee the process for managing case meetings.

When a family or individual is causing a nuisance a preliminary meeting is held to review the case. This is followed by a case conference (attended by all relevant agencies and the subject of the meeting). The Case Conference agrees an action plan to resolve the anti social behaviour. The action plan may include legal action, an Acceptable Behaviour Contract or interventions offering support to the alleged perpetrator and/or victims of nuisance.

The City Council is currently improving this approach by establishing a multi-agency Anti Social Behaviour Unit. The Unit will co-ordinate this process centrally and will ensure that the city's response to nuisance is clear and consistent

4.41   But for too long there have been circumstances around the country where local authorities have been re-housing families over and over, despite evidence and a history of anti-social behaviour. Often, authorities have felt obliged to accept these families as homeless and in priority need because they have children, and re-house them automatically. This is not effective for two reasons. Firstly nothing is done to make the family or individual change their behaviour and secondly, it undermines the confidence and security of communities who have had their lives made a misery, and who have had the courage to take action and stand up as witnesses.

4.42   Through the Homelessness Act 2002, we have revised the housing legislation so that, local authorities now have a specific power to refuse to allocate social housing to any household which is guilty of unacceptable behaviour serious enough to make them unsuitable as tenants. Additionally, local authorities must treat any household that becomes homeless as a result of their own anti-social behaviour as 'intentionally homeless'. This means that the help they can get is limited to advice and assistance. If the household includes children or vulnerable people, they will also be entitled to a short period of temporary accommodation, but only for long enough to give them a reasonable chance to find alternative accommodation for themselves. These limitations on the help available to households who make themselves homeless through their own bad behaviour are made clear in statutory guidance on homelessness and housing allocations issued recently to local authorities.

4.43   Some landlords take no interest in their tenants' behaviour. Properties are not kept in good keep, rubbish is often dumped anywhere and everywhere and tenants who are behaving anti-socially get away with it because their rent is simply paid direct to a landlord. In this situation no-one takes responsibility. The fact that some social rented tenants move into the private sector after they have been evicted can also create problems.

4.44   The forthcoming Housing Bill will provide discretionary powers for the selective licensing by local authorities of private landlords in areas of low housing demand.

4.45   In areas subject to selective licensing, landlords will need to be 'fit and proper persons' (no criminal convictions) or appoint agents who are. They will need to meet minimum management standards and play their part in dealing with anti-social tenants and by taking up references. In England, local housing authorities will, with the approval of the Secretary of State, be able to designate an area as subject to selective licensing if:

(a)   the area is an area of low housing demand, or is likely to become an area of low housing demand if it is not designated; and

(b)   the designation will, when considered together with other measures being taken in the area by the local housing authority, contribute to the improvement of the social or economic conditions in the area.

4.46   In addition to this, in the forthcoming Housing Bill new powers will be introduced to enable local authorities to licence areas where there are problems with the private rented sector to target problem landlords. Landlords who are unfit to manage their property will not be licenced and will have housing benefit payments withdrawn.

4.47   The Government strongly believes in the principle of a welfare state, which is based on rights and responsibilities. Those who behave anti-socially within their home and neighbourhood, making life miserable for the rest of the community, are abusing the support they receive from society through Housing Benefit.

4.48   We will be consulting on whether to give local authorities an enabling power to withhold payments of Housing Benefit to individual tenants where they believe this is the most effective way of tackling anti-social behaviour. This will include a look at introducing an automatic trigger for Housing Benefit sanctions either in designated geographical areas where this is a problem or once individual anti-social behaviour has reached a particular level and requires enforcement action.

4.49   These measures, as appropriate, would apply to those funded directly by Government, including the National Asylum Support Service and the contracting landlords.

4.50   It is important that anti-social behaviour is tackled no matter where people live. This includes owner-occupiers. The enforcement mechanisms, such as injunctions and ASBOs will be used in any area. It is important that in any area where anti-social behaviour is identified as a major problem local authorities should consider establishing specialist anti-social behaviour units. There are excellent examples across the country where this has happened to the benefit of the whole community.

4.51   As outlined in Chapter Two, it is vitally important to ensure that help is offered to families or individuals that are behaving anti-socially. All the interventions such as parenting or family support, special schemes to help families who are behaving antisocially as well as warnings, acceptable behaviour contracts, injunctions are absolutely vital to the above processes and need to be in place. But we must also ensure that clear and swift enforcement action is taken when necessary.

4.52   Later this month the Office of the Deputy Prime Minister will be publishing a study on tackling anti-social behaviour in mixed tenure areas. The study looked at 'what works' and how barriers to implementing effective anti-social behaviour strategies can be overcome.

Neighbourhood Renewal Partnerships

4.53   At the heart of this Government's determination to tackle social exclusion is the National Strategy for Neighbourhood Renewal. That strategy must tackle and reduce the incidence and perception of anti-social behaviour if the Government is to achieve its aims of revitalising the most deprived communities. Communities drive this agenda. It is Government's role to empower them to succeed. That is why:

- Since 2001 the Government has invested heavily in Neighbourhood Renewal areas. Over £2 billion over the next 10 years is for the New Deal for Communities partnerships.
- We are providing £36 million through the Community Empowerment Fund to help communities get involved in local decision-making, and a further combined £60 million for community chests and community learning chests to support small community projects with grants they can get locally with minimum bureaucracy.
- 84 neighbourhood warden schemes and 123 street warden initiatives, supported with a total of £100 million, are now operating across England and Wales.

- A new £22.5 million Street Crime Warden initiative was announced in June 2002. The programme funds 38 schemes with 368 wardens, and increases the number of wardens in areas where there is a high level of street crime.
- The Neighbourhood Renewal Fund provides the 88 most deprived wards in the country with funds to improve services investing £300 million in 2002/03, £400 million in 2003/04, £450 million in 2004/05, and £525 million in 2005/06.

4.54   Tackling anti-social behaviour is critical to our success in empowering deprived neighbourhoods and communities. The stakes are very high not only in human terms but also financially. In the East Manchester New Deal for Communities area, they took decisive action against two people who were ruining the area. After they managed to secure ASBOs against them the takings in the local supermarket increased by £4,000 a week as people came back into the area both to live and shop.

4.55   Much of the best practice adopted by local authorities and the police across the country is funded by our Neighbourhood Renewal Unit set up in 1999. This investment and the strategy make a huge difference to our ability to tackle anti-social behaviour across the country. We need to ensure by working with the CDRPs and with local authorities, Government Offices and others that these partnerships deliver on the action to tackle anti social behaviour.

Government Offices

4.56   The Government Offices in the Regions have an important role to play in supporting and monitoring local delivery. Effective interventions to address and prevent anti-social behaviour needs to cover, for example, housing, environment, community policies, neighbourhood renewal and regeneration, and link with work to reduce crime and disorder, where the Government Offices in the Regions already co-ordinate initiatives and manage relevant funding streams.

Sustainable Communities

4.57   Earlier this year we also published *Substantial Communities: Building for the Future* which outlined a comprehensive long-term programme of action to create better quality housing, better design, better local environment, better use of land and planning, better public transport and better use of public investment. It includes a package of funding totalling £22 billion over the next three years. It will be a key element in our drive to tackle anti-social behaviour.

Resident and Community Groups

4.58   Community groups such as tenants or residents' organisations make a real difference to anti-social behaviour being tackled successfully. Local people must be encouraged to win back their communities and supported by local and central Government to do so.

4.59   In January this year, the Government published ''Crime Reduction Basics'', a training package for use by community groups and individuals www.crimereduction.gov.uk/learningzone/crimereductionbasics.htm.
The pack is designed to introduce individuals and groups in the community to the basic principles of crime and disorder reduction and to encourage them to get involved in reducing crime, especially anti-social behaviour. The pack contains actual case studies of projects where communities have successfully tackled anti-social behaviour problems in their neighbourhoods.

> **Cottington Close Estate Management Board** has adopted a 'Good Neighbour Declaration' to take a stand against anti-social behaviour. The declaration sets out responsibilities for the landlord, how they will deal with complaints and the legal action they are willing to use. The residents also sign up to conduct themselves properly and look after the local environment. Many residents have signed the declaration and have contributed to improving the quality of life for local residents.

4.60   The critical role that residents, tenants, Neighbourhood Watch or other community groups can provide is also one of supporting and empowering them to deal with these problems day after day. Knowing that other people are sympathetic and want to help can often be the first and most important step for anyone to come forward and begin to seek help.

> **Neighbourhood Watch**
>
> Neighbourhood Watch schemes have a central role to play in the fight against crime. There is clear evidence that individual schemes have brought about significant reductions in certain types of crime, especially burglary. In addition – and just as importantly – it can significantly reduce the fear of crime, and help to rebuild community spirit. There are now about 160,000 Neighbourhood Watch schemes in England and Wales covering six million households. The Home Office supports these projects with, for example, a detailed training manual for scheme co-ordinators.

4.61   It can often be one person who can be the catalyst for change. This can be a Housing Estate Manager, a Fire-Officer, a Community Beat Officer, an Environmental Health Officer, a special constable or a member of the public in no 'official' capacity.

The Cowley Estate in Lambeth

The Housing Estate Manager was the key catalyst for the Cowley Estate in Lambeth. A thorough estate inspection was carried out in partnership with the police and a surveyor. An Action Plan was drawn up and circulated to residents. Garages used by drug dealers were demolished, bushes and hedges cut down to increase visibility and CCTV introduced. The local community fought – and won – a legal battle to close down a pub in the area, which had been identified as a key drug-dealing location. Residents who made others' lives a misery were "named and shamed" in newsletters and in the media.

4.62   But although it is important for local people to do all they can to help themselves, it is also important that the authorities do not abdicate responsibility for problems and that they take decisive and appropriate action. They need to support the work of residents. For example, this support could be to provide a telephone, meeting room or computer to residents to enable them to produce a newsletter, auditing the extent of anti-social problems on estates. It could be by lending or buying hand held cameras or diaries so people can collect information on problems. It could simply be a matter of responding to some of the requests for rubbish clearance outside of the normal cycles for collection.

4.63   The Government recognises the importance of helping to build the capacity of people and community groups to participate more in achieving change in their communities. The Active Community Unit has led a review of Government action in this area, and will be making recommendations to ensure that Government programmes and funding streams which support community capacity building are more coherent and effective in the future

Protecting and Empowering Local People

4.64   Local residents are often at the centre of any action taken against people behaving anti-socially, either because they experience it day after day, or because they are witnesses. Although it is now possible for hearsay evidence or professional witnesses to be used it is nevertheless important for individuals and their communities to take control of their own environment, to speak out, and for their words to be acted upon in a way that gives them protection from retribution. Those that are intimidating witnesses need to be dealt with severely by the courts as an example to others and to give confidence to those brave enough to stand up to them. The police, courts and others should always give the utmost thought to the potential vulnerability of witnesses in any proceedings.

4.65   The Government in turn is reviewing all aspects of support given to witnesses. A national strategy for victims and witnesses is being developed and will be published shortly and we will be publishing guidance on witness intimidation this summer. The draft Victims of Crime Bill will also be published shortly which will propose the establishment of a new Commissioner for Victims and Witnesses, to be a national voice for their interests.

4.66   Victims and witnesses need support both in the community, and at court. Intimidation is an offence, which can carry a serious penalty, and we need to ensure that offenders are dealt with promptly and effectively. The police provide protection in very serious cases.

4.67   Social landlords have a crucial role to play, and can use injunctions and eviction procedures against tenants who intimidate. They can also re-house victims and witnesses both in serious cases and in cases of lower level repeat victimisation which can create serious psychological harm. We will work with social landlords to develop best practice and ensure that people at risk are fast tracked to appropriate accommodation.

4.68   A range of measures for vulnerable and intimidated witness have recently been introduced into criminal proceedings and we will review how best to ensure their application in anti-social behaviour order hearings.

4.69   A number of pilots are being run by the Courts Service, Police and Crown Prosecution Service to improve case administration, reduce the number of cases that do not take place on the appointed day, and improve communication with and information for witnesses. We will identify and apply the lessons from the pilots.

4.70   The Witness Service, run by the national voluntary organisation Victim Support, recently extended their service to Magistrates' Courts, and we will work with them and the courts administration to ensure that those giving evidence in ASBO hearings will be able to benefit form the advice and support they provide. The Courts Service has a rolling programme to introduce separate facilities for prosecution and defence witnesses, and victims and witnesses in ASBO hearings will benefit from these.

Witness case study

On an estate in the Midlands, a group regularly intimidated and harassed local people. The group would stand outside the witnesses' house, shout abuse and refuse to move out of the way when people came to visit. When the witness went to the shops they would follow her, swearing and shouting, and throw mud and stones at her and her property.
The behaviour of this group affected a wide area. Several residents moved away, rather than challenge the offenders – one resident moved in and out of a property in the area within 24 hours.

> Despite local people living in fear of reprisals, sufficient evidence was gathered to place an Anti-Social Behaviour Order on the ringleader. Two days after it was granted, the Order was breached. Three witnesses gave evidence of the breach, but only one of those witnesses was confident enough to come to court. As a result of this witness coming forward the offender received a 2-year Supervision Order for the breach of the ASBO. When they breached the Supervision Order the offender then received a custodial sentence.

4.71   The people who have had the courage to come forward and bear witness deserve support. So we also intend to recognise the courage of people who do so by the introduction of a Community Awards Scheme for individuals or small groups who tried to make a difference. Details of this will be announced later in the year.

4.72   Once the fear of reprisal is removed, tenant, resident or community groups can play a vital role as a catalyst locally to hold the police, local authorities and all the partnerships to account for action against anti-social behaviour. There are many examples of good work around the country – small groups are given portable hand held cameras as well as diaries to capture evidence of the perpetrators. Other people are connected up to police stations with panic buttons to give them support during long criminal proceedings. Some local councillors hire community, church halls or their offices to collect evidence away from the street where the problems are. We will encourage and roll out this good practice.

Fire Service

4.73   The Fire Service also has a strong record of partnership working to help reduce anti-social behaviour by young people, through outreach and direct intervention initiatives. This work is designed to help combat anti-social behaviour by young people towards firefighters on operational duty and the wider community in general.

> ### Fire Service Initiatives
> - Young Firefighters Association – a uniformed youth organisation run by around 40 fire brigades across the country that provide fire safety training, physical activities and a disciplined environment for 11-16 year olds. Members are intentionally recruited from lower socio-economic areas and young offenders.
> - We are wholly or part funding 46 local arson prevention pilot projects throughout England and Wales, costing just over £2 million. Projects include local Arson Task Forces, where fire & police services and local authorities jointly target arson 'hotspots' by a mixture of youth education programmes, swiftly clearing fly-tipped rubbish & abandoned cars and boarding-up empty properties.

Public transport providers and police

4.74   Anti-social behaviour on and around public transport can have a significant impact on people's decisions to use public transport, through fear of crime on the route to, and while waiting for, public transport as well as a cost to transport operators from for example, vandalism and graffiti.

4.75   The Social Exclusion Unit's report 'Making the connections: Final report on Transport and Social Exclusion' sets out the framework for a new process of accessibility planning. Accessibility planning will bring together local transport authorities and key partners such as CDRPs, to identify and tackle the barriers to people's access to key services, including anti-social behaviour. The Government will issue guidance on accessibility planning, and will encourage co-operation between transport providers and CDRPs.

4.76   The Government has promoted initiatives such as the Secure Stations Scheme; a national accreditation scheme recognising set standards of good practice in rail station, staff and passenger security. The Government has also set up a new "Safer Travel on Buses and Coaches Panel" to look at ways to combat crime on buses and coaches in England and to create a safe environment for crews and passengers.

4.77   The British Transport Police have a key role in combating anti-social behaviour on buses, trains and tubes. That is why, in the Police Reform Act 2002, we gave them the power to apply for Anti-Social Behaviour Orders.

British Transport Police Project

In the first scheme of its kind a local partnership organisation is funding two additional British Transport Police Officers to patrol the Finsbury Park area.

With the agreement of the Metropolitan Police, who are part of the Finsbury Park Partnership group, the officers will go beyond their normal rail and Underground remit to patrol the area within a half-mile radius of Finsbury Park station.

The new beat officers have been brought in, as the area has traditionally been the responsibility of three separate Borough-based police divisions of the Metropolitan Police (Hackney, Haringey and Islington) with BTP and the station at its heart. Because of this division of responsibility the area has not always been policed in a holistic way.

Now, they are working with local communities to solve the area's crime and disorder problems. The Finsbury Park Partnership has already funded a number of other Crime Reduction initiatives in the Finsbury Park area including:

- Setting-up an 8-camera CCTV system around the Finsbury Park station
- A victim support scheme
- A youth inclusion project
- A drugs education project
- Street light improvements in back streets

- Target hardening measures for the homes of vulnerable individuals living in the area

Graffiti Unit

The British Transport Police Graffiti Unit is based in Stockwell South London. It has found that graffiti offences diminish when the leaders of known graffiti gangs are apprehended. The Graffiti Unit has a computer database within which details of all known tags and offenders are logged, this assists in identifying persistent offenders and graffiti hotspots. The Graffiti Unit is a "hub" nationally, for the gathering and distribution of graffiti related information for all Metropolitan Police Boroughs and County forces.

The business community

4.78   Local businesses have an important role in tackling anti-social behaviour and in making sure they do not cause it themselves – from football clubs running programmes to tackle racism to retailers improving their local environment and keeping it clear from vandalism, littering and graffiti.

4.79   National businesses can play their part. For example, cable company 'boxes' are often targets for graffiti 'tags' and there have been issues over liability when councils have tried to clean these. Agreements should be reached over this issue to allow councils free access to clean such 'boxes', unless businesses will commit to their own cleaning regime.

Adshel

Adshel provide a variety of 'street furniture', including bus shelters, interactive kiosks, information panels and automatic public toilets. Across the UK Adshel has 28,507 roadside structures, the vast majority of which are bus shelters.

Adshel has experienced increased levels of shelter vandalism and graffiti over the last few years across the country. In 2002 66,000 pieces of graffiti and flyposting were removed nationally.

Adshel has introduced a 24-hour a day damage hotline and responds immediately to reports of offensive graffiti and to make shelters safe. In Cardiff alone, Adshel spends £100,000 every year maintaining and repairing shelters.

In South Wales, Adshel is working with Youth Works (a cooperation between Groundwork, Crime Concern and Marks & Spencer) on a scheme in a Bridgend housing estate. The scheme aims to achieve a 30-50% reduction in neighbourhood crime within 3 years, through working with young people on the estate. Activities include preventative work, diversionary work such as sports skills and remedial and community work aimed at young people. A survey is currently underway to ask young people in the area why they think people in their age group commit vandalism. Adshel is currently working with Cardiff County Council on an initiative to install CCTV cameras on a number of bus shelters later this year and to monitor the effects on shelter damage.

4.80   Businesses are part of communities and can be victims of anti-social behaviour. Vandalism and graffiti drive customers away from local shops, which in turn can lead to businesses relocating, taking jobs away. They themselves have a role to play in tackling or preventing anti-social behaviour, for example they should not sell alcohol to underage young people and children. Local businesses are important partners in CDRPs and key to practical, local solutions.

4.81   In many town centres and shopping precincts businesses have come together often with their Local Authorities acting as catalyst, to appoint and fund a Town Centre Manager, who will pull together activity to improve the town centre trading environment. The Association of Town Centre Management (www.atcm.org) provides checklists and guidance on how to set up these types of initiatives. Effective town centre initiatives cover a range of issues, many of which impact directly on anti-social behaviour, including:

- Improving lighting in communal areas;
- Installing CCTV;
- 'Shop Watch' schemes to tackle shoplifters;
- Improving the look of vacant shops with murals/displays to reduce them being targets for graffiti;
- Improving the ambience and safety of car parks;
- Appoint litter rangers to augment existing services;
- Providing street environment enhancements such as new street furniture and the greening of town centres with appropriate planting;
- Encouraging community celebrations, such as fayres and themed events.

4.82   On 24 April 2001 the Government announced its intention to introduce Business Improvement Districts (BIDs) in England. BIDs will allow Local Authorities and local businesses to work together to put in place local projects to improve their area. Projects could cover a wide variety of issues including improvements to the quality of the local environment, the street environment, or parks and open spaces. It could pay for measures such as CCTV or warden schemes. There would be a "contract" between Local Authorities and local businesses for additional services or improvements, funded by a levy raised through an additional rate.

4.83   The Office of the Deputy Prime Minister's interim guidance on BIDs was launched in January 2003 and provides practical information and advice to businesses and councils wanting to set up a BID their local area. The guidance is available on the ODPM website at www.local-regions.odpm.gov.uk/bids/index.htm. Also in January a pilot project of 22 BIDs was announced. The programme, being co-ordinated by the Association of Town Centre Management, will ensure that once legislation is passed, as is expected in the course of

2003, these pilots will be able to 'go live' immediately. The pilot programme will also provide knowledge to the private and public sectors on how to set up a BID and will also be used to update the interim guidance by providing lessons learnt

CHAPTER FOUR: SUMMARY OF NEW MEASURES

Crime and Disorder Reduction Partnerships

- CDRP strategies will include action to tackle anti-social behaviour.

Police

- National Policing Plan makes tackling anti-social behaviour a key priority.
- There are now more police officers than at any time in history, we are on track to reach our target of 132,500 by 2004.
- The Home Office will work with police forces and local authorities to ensure that Community Safety Accreditation Schemes are set up throughout England and Wales.
- We will extend Fixed Penalty Notice powers for disorder to accredited persons.

Tackling anti-social behaviour in housing

- Social landlords will be required to publish their policies and procedures on anti-social behaviour.
- All social landlords will now have the same powers as Local Authorities to obtain county court injunctions which can exclude perpetrators of anti-social behaviour from a specified area and if necessary their home.
- Changes to injunctions will also widen the range of people who can be protected from the perpetrators of anti-social behaviour.
- We will also enable Housing Action Trusts to apply directly for ASBOs so that they too have greater scope for tackling anti-social behaviour.
- Anti social tenants will lose their secured or assured tenancies and be demoted to probationary tenancies until their behaviour is addressed. They will lose their right to buy.
- Social Landlords will also be able to extend the initial 12 month period of the introductory, starter or probationary tenancy by a further 6 months if they have concern about behaviour.
- Courts will now have to consider the impact of anti-social behaviour on individual victims and the wider community in all housing possession cases.
- The forthcoming Housing Bill will provide discretionary powers for the selective licensing by local authorities of private landlords in areas of low housing demand.
- The Housing Bill will also introduce new powers to enable local authorities to licence areas where there are problems with the private landlords. Those who are unfit to manage their property will not be licenced and will have housing benefit withdrawn.
- We will also be consulting with local authorities on whether to give them an enabling power to withhold payments of housing benefit to tenants where they believe this is the most effective way of tackling anti-social behaviour.

Protecting and Empowering People

- A national strategy for victims and witnesses is also being developed and a draft Victims Of Crime Bill will be published shortly.
- We intend to recognise the courage of witnesses by the introduction of a Community Awards Scheme for individuals or small groups who have tried to make a difference.

Chapter Five

EFFECTIVE ENFORCEMENT

5.1   It is important for communities to set the standards of behaviour by which they expect people to live. But if these standards are to be credible and respected, it must be clear to everyone that swift and effective action will be taken against unacceptable behaviour. This action must be unfettered by unnecessary bureaucracy. The processes need to be transparent and accessible to the community and the needs of victims must be central.

5.2   We all have a responsibility to adhere to acceptable standards of behaviour, both as individuals and in our families. Some matters need to be enforced in a more formal way. Environmental health officers, educational welfare officers, housing officers, social workers, the police, Community Support Officers and others already have powers that enable them to tackle many forms of anti-social behaviour.

5.3   This White Paper and the forthcoming Bill are designed to bring forward urgent and important measures that will build on what already works or develop new ways of tackling problems. In some instances we need to introduce new measures to ensure local authorities,the police the judicial system and others have the right powers. But, equally, we need to support and encourage agencies to use the powers already available to them to deliver on their responsibility to contribute to the reduction of anti-social behaviour. This chapter sets out a revised and strengthened framework of interventions that will ensure:

- That the **right powers** are in place and
- That they are available to the **right people.**
- That these powers are **straightforward and speedy** to use.
- That should one intervention not be effective, **others** are available

The more that can be done to enforce standards without resorting to the courts the more effective action is. However, where court action is necessary it should be taken swiftly. There are various stages at which different levels of intervention and enforcement are appropriate according to the persistent nature of the offending.

Fixed Penalty Notices

5.4   FPNs are the first stage for most forms of low level disorder offences. They offer speedy and effective action that frees up police and court time. The offender receives an immediate punishment, which if paid, will not result in a criminal record.

5.5   The Criminal Justice and Police Act 2001 provided the police with new powers to issue FPNs to those aged 18 years or older, for 11 specified offences, including being drunk and disorderly, throwing fireworks, and causing harassment, alarm or distress.

5.6   Pilot schemes are progressing successfully in four areas (West Midlands, Essex, Croydon and North Wales). As of 5 January 2003 a total of 1835 FPNs had been issued. An overall payment rate of 60% is being achieved and only 2% are ending up in court.

5.7   We will build on these schemes to introduce FPNs that will bring benefits to the local community in terms of reducing anti-social behaviour. We will be consulting with police forces, including the British Transport Police, to see whether FPNs are needed for other offences.

5.8   The Police Reform Act 2002 extended the power to issue FPNs for disorder to community support officers. The Anti-Social Behaviour Bill will extend these powers to other persons accredited by the Chief Constable. Accredited persons such as local authority officers are already be able to issue FPNs for litter under the Environmental Protection Act. We are expanding these powers so that local authorities and other accredited persons can issue FPNs for a wider range of offences related to environmental quality, such as fly-posting or graffiti. The Bill will also close an existing loophole so that Community Support Officers can effectively tackle the nuisance of people cycling on the pavement.

5.9   At present FPNs can only be issued to people over 18. We will pilot the FPN scheme for disorder offences to 16-17 year olds who will be made responsible for paying their own fines.

Current Fixed Penalty Notices for disorder (Criminal Justice and Police Act 2001)	
Wasting police time	£80
Sending false (hoax) messages	£80
Knowingly giving a false alarm to the fire brigade	£80
Causing harassment alarm or distress	£80
Drunk and Disorderly	£40
Trespass on a railway	£40
Throwing stones at a train	£40
Drunk on a highway	£40
Buying alcohol for an under 18	£40
Throwing fireworks	£40
Drinking in a designated public area	£40

Warnings

5.10   Written verbal warnings can be very effective in stopping people behaving anti-socially. Good practice is that the police or local authority explain to individuals, children or their parents what the problem is and the consequences of their behaviour. In many cases the threat of an ASBO has proved a sufficient deterrent.

5.11   Warnings generally describe the behaviour observed, inform the individual that the behaviour is anti-social and unacceptable, advise them that their behaviour is being monitored and warn that an ASBO will be sought if the behaviour continues. Where appropriate referrals are also made to support organisations specialising, for example, in tenancy support, family services or counselling.

Westminster Warnings

The City of Westminster in conjunction with the Metropolitan Police use warning letters as an initial intervention for those who are committing anti-social acts, including drug and prostitution related activities. The warning letters explicitly state that if the individual concerned does not cease their behaviour the council will apply for an ASBO to protect the community. The warning letter is accompanied by details of support services relating to the individual's specific needs.

Acceptable Behaviour Contracts

5.12   Islington Borough Council Housing Department and Islington Borough Police initiated the idea of an 'Acceptable Behaviour Contract' (ABC) – a written, voluntary agreement between an individual, the local housing office and the police. Crucially, the police and council do not have to apply to a court and consequently acceptable behaviour contracts are a quick, flexible response to anti-social behaviour.

5.13   There has been much take up of ABCs around the country. As of April 2002, there were around 200 ABC schemes in England and Wales with at least 1800 contracts made.

5.14   ABC's are flexible and can be used for a variety of situations with adults as well as young people. Problems dealt with include truanting, vandalism, neighbour nuisance, bullying and unacceptable drinking. Schemes specifically for adults have targeted kerb-crawlers, ex-offenders leaving prison and neighbour disputes.

5.15   Interventions such as ABCs and ASBOs are rarely used in isolation. More often they form part of a coherent strategy to tackle anti-social behaviour. Although there are cases where an immediate application for an ASBO is appropriate, there are other cases where practitioners will consider an ABC to be the correct intervention. It is of course vital that any breach of an ABC is enforced by further action such as an ASBO.

Southampton ABCs

Southampton council's acceptable behaviour contract (ABC) scheme has been running for approximately 2 years and around 120 contracts have been issued, the majority of them with juveniles. The success of the ABC scheme has meant that only 10 ASBOs have been required in the city. In one instance where a young man had been seriously harassing the residents of a sheltered housing scheme an ABC was successfully completed and the residents gave him a gift for staying out of trouble.

Injunctions

5.16   A wide range of injunctions are available and being used by local authorities to tackle anti-social behaviour. Injunctions are flexible and fast – a court can make an injunction within hours of a complaint and before the problem escalates. In Birmingham injunctions have been used along with other measures to tackle the effects of street prostitution in local communities, particularly within the Edgbaston and Ladywood areas. In one case, successful legal action was been taken against 20 street workers under the Highways Act 1980 to prevent soliciting and loitering in any road, street or highway for the purpose of prostitution. In Manchester 300 to 400 housing injunctions are used each year to protect individuals where there has been violence or the threat of violence. In Bristol the local authority reports a significant and visible reduction in aggressive begging, which is tackled by injunctions made on the basis of trespass and vagrancy laws. See further information on the Bristol City Council Street Wise Project in Chapter Three.

Anti-Social Behaviour Orders

5.17   The Government introduced ASBOs in the Crime and Disorder Act 1998 to tackle low level criminal and sub-criminal behaviour. ASBOs are civil orders that exist to protect the public from behaviour which causes harassment, alarm or distress. An order can prohibit the offender from specific anti-social acts or from entering defined areas and is effective for a minimum of two years. The consequences of breaching an ASBO are a maximum penalty of 5 years in prison.

5.18   In response to concerns of people in local communities as well as local authorities, the police and social landlords the Government introduced radical improvements to ASBOs under the Police Reform Act 2002. The Act introduced interim orders, orders on conviction in criminal courts and orders in county court proceedings, enabled the British Transport Police and registered social landlords to apply for ASBOs and extended the area an ASBO can cover to any defined part or the whole of England and Wales. These changes were accompanied by new Home Office guidance.

5.19   Communities are already experiencing the benefits as agencies on the ground use their new powers. Interim orders in particular are already widely in use across the country and orders have also been made to stop individuals from anti-social acts across the whole of England and Wales. Many agencies are also utilising orders on conviction powers by ensuring that as well as the court punishing an offender the community is protected from their anti-social behaviour.

> **Providing swift protection to the community using interim orders**
>
> The elderly residents of a supported housing scheme in Wirral were frequently kept awake by excessive noise and loud shouting in the early hours of the morning by a man in his 30s who was staying in one of the bungalows with his mother. The residents were increasingly disturbed and frightened by the man's behaviour.
>
> The council obtained an interim order against the man. It was made without advance notice being given to him and came into effect when it was served on him the next day. The terms of the order were comprehensive. The order prohibited the man from using threatening abusive or insulting language, using or threatening violence, playing music or listening to a television set at an excessively loud volume between 10pm and 9am, or acting in a drunken or disorderly manner.
>
> The man was arrested for an alleged breach on the same day the order was served. The following day he was remanded in custody for 7 days charged with breaching the order. The full hearing for an ASBO was scheduled for a few weeks later.
>
> The interim order and the immediate action in response to its breach have restored the residents' faith in the local police. The community have been reassured that such orders and any breaches are taken seriously and provide them with immediate protection.

5.20   Orders on conviction remove the need for a separate hearing in a different court, which means that the public can be protected from anti-social behaviour without delay. However, to make an order the court must have the right information. Clear roles, in particular, that of the Crown Prosecution Service (CPS), and partnership working are vital. Protocols between the CPS and the police will be developed to ensure that criminal courts have the evidence needed to make an order on conviction.

5.21   Another measure which enables the community to be protected against anti-social behaviour at the earliest possible opportunity are orders in the county court. From April, county courts will be able to use their new powers under the Police Reform Act 2002 to make orders against defendants who are appearing in related proceedings. To make best use of court time we will extend this power further so that when a tenant is being evicted, for example, due to the anti-social behaviour of a family member or friend the court can also make an order against the person responsible for the anti-social behaviour. This avoids the need for the same evidence to be presented in a different court to obtain the ASBO, hence reducing the burden on witnesses.

5.22   Currently, local authorities, police forces and registered social landlords who have used ASBOs to protect people against the nuisance caused by a young person are often excluded from court when the order is breached. It is important that agencies have access to the court in these cases. We will take steps to ensure that applicant agencies who have obtained orders have automatic access to breach prosecutions in the youth court to monitor the case and keep witnesses and victims informed.

5.23   Breach of an ASBO is a criminal offence, which at present is only prosecuted by the Crown Prosecution Service. Local authorities have requested the power to prosecute breaches of orders obtained by them. Local authorities are already able to prosecute certain offences such as environmental infringements and we will extend this to allow local authorities to prosecute breach of ASBOs.

5.24   Effective sentencing for breach of an ASBO is essential for the orders to have any value. We will work with the Magistrates Association and the Judicial Studies Board to ensure that there is a consistent response to the sentencing of the breach of ASBOs. When an order is breached it is vital that the court is aware of the impact of the anti-social behaviour on victims and the wider community. To achieve this, prosecutors should liaise with the appropriate agency to arrange for them to give factual information to the court after conviction about the circumstances in which the ASBO was applied for and granted and the context within which the present breach offence took place.

Community accountability

5.25   Appropriate publicity of action taken is a key part of any strategy to tackle anti-social behaviour. It provides reassurance to local residents that the authorities are taking action and, where orders are made, it enables people to identify breaches. Publicity of an order sends out a clear message that anti-social behaviour will not be tolerated. We will therefore remove automatic reporting restrictions on orders made on conviction in the youth court.

5.26   The Government is developing new proposals to pilot 'Community Justice Centres' that will improve links between the community and the delivery of justice. The pilots would be able to deal with all low-level disorder offences, housing related matters, especially those relevant to tackling anti-social behaviour. Those who adjudicate would receive specialist training. The aim would be to facilitate better liaison and communication with the courts, thereby reducing delays in the listing of cases and producing more consistent breach sentencing due to increased awareness of local issues and the impact of the anti-social behaviour. They would also give fast access to alternatives to custody such as treatment for drug misuse, debt counselling, reparation to the community with immediate commencement .

5.27   In addition to considering new ideas, we must also strengthen existing structures. It is absolutely vital that courts and magistrates have credibility with local people and that their sentencing follows the overall judicial guidelines and is appropriate to local circumstances as well as the personal circumstances of the offender. Rights of the community must be balanced with those of the offender and victims. Decisions that ignore this principle risk letting down the public and making witnesses even more reluctant to come forward.

Better information for magistrates

Coventry City Council and its partners have worked very hard to ensure that magistrates locally have a full understanding of what anti social behaviour is doing to their local community. This included a seminar for magistrates and a video using footage taken by professional witnesses on local estates. This enabled the magistrates to better understand the serious impact of anti-social behaviour on local people. The video is now widely used in training sessions for neighbourhood wardens, local authority officers, the police and others.

5.28   The Judicial Studies Board has developed a training package for magistrates to develop their understanding of anti-social behaviour and the sentencing options available to them.

Innovative work in Cardiff

In 2002 Cardiff County Council introduced a number of changes to ensure that key operational staff within the council and the police were confident about tackling anti-social behaviour. They developed a four stage process for handling complaints, problem solving interventions and enforcement. The police and council reviewed how they had been collecting data on anti-social behaviour and created new data analysis systems. This enables them to target problem areas and perpetrators. A training course was also developed for councillors, officials, police officers and social housing landlords. Seven courses for 180 staff have already been run and further courses are to run throughout 2003.

Within weeks of the first training sessions, 5 ASBOs were successfully applied for by staff who had attended courses and now more ASBO applications are being processed. In addition, better multi-agency interventions are stopping anti-social behaviour before legal action is necessary. The final part of the strategy is about to be implemented – the CPS is providing a dedicated ASBO solicitor to provide early advice on evidence for orders and prosecuting breaches.

Making fines more effective

5.29   Currently, the success rate for the collection of fines is around 60%. The Lord Chancellor's Department is taking a number of initiatives to improve this, including the provision of extra resources through using the income from fines to invest in fine enforcement activity; direct contact with fine defaulters so as to determine underlying reasons. However, there is a clear need to tackle structural weaknesses in the system. The Courts Bill, currently before Parliament, includes a package of measures to improve enforcement, which will be piloted before nationwide introduction. These measures include:

- A discount for prompt payment in line with agreed terms, or Increases if the defendant fails to pay on time, or fails to contact the court to reschedule payments;
- Fines officers to manage the collection and enforcement of outstanding financial penalties. They would have power to adjust payment terms (but not to alter the level of the fine) as well as powers to impose a range of sanctions, where defendants can pay but won't pay, including:
  - Registering the fine with the registry of judgements (which would make it difficult for defaulters to obtain credit);
  - Ordering the clamping of a vehicle, which could be sold if the fine was not paid;
  - Authorising bailiffs to seize defaulters' goods;
  - Ordering deductions to be made from defaulters' pay or benefits.

5.30   The ability of the Fine Officer to deduct fines from salaries or benefits will contribute to restoring the community's faith in the fines system. We also want to look at a range of different ways to ensure that fines are paid to increase confidence in fining as a sentence.

Restorative justice

5.31   Communities need to see the impact of offenders brought to justice, not only through a reduction in offending but also by directly benefiting from community punishments. For example, the perpetrators should clean up graffiti and those who have committed acts of vandalism should make good the damage.

5.32   Restorative justice ensures that punishment for an offence is accountable and responsive to the wider community. This includes working in the community, bringing together the victim and the offender or wider victim support work. It helps offenders understand that their offending behaviour is not just against the law, but also has a damaging effect on their victims, themselves and on their communities.

5.33   Restorative justice also gives a voice to victims by bringing them into the process and involving them in the solution. Volunteers from the public can be recruited to act as mediators or sit on community panels. And within restorative conferences, they can represent the community viewpoint or attend in a personal capacity to support the individual offender or victim. The Youth Justice Board has developed this for young people. Young offenders have to agree a contract which requires them, along with their parents, to tackle their offending behaviour and make amends to their victim or the wider community.

5.34   As part of the Government's approach to restorative justice strategy, we will:

- consider the availability of restorative justice across all age groups and at all stages of the criminal process: pre-crime, especially with juveniles, pre-charge, post conviction/pre sentence, and post sentence
- make the link with work to turn children away from crime for instance through funding informal panels in schools and other institutions to tackle bullying and anti-social behaviour
- give a high priority to the needs of victims (research suggests that victims who participate in restorative processes find it a positive experience)
- seek to maximise the potential of restorative justice to reduce re-offending
- promote consistent, appropriate and effective use of restorative justice techniques

5.35   All YOTs are required to organise 'Community Payback' to ensure that young people on Reparation Orders repay their debt to the community. The purpose of 'Community Payback' is to prevent offending by bringing home to young people the consequences of their behaviour and enabling them to make amends, as appropriate, either to their victims or the wider community or to both. YOTs must now ensure that restorative processes are used in 100% of Referral Orders and at least 75% of other YOT interventions.

Operation Blizzard is a Gateshead-based project to tackle crime, anti-social behaviour and substance misuse. Seven young people, aged between 13 and 17, helped in the re-decoration of the project's building — in some cases painting over their own graffiti. Their offending had included burglary, assault and driving offences. All completed their reparation programme and learnt new skills. Two of the young people enjoyed it so much that they chose to help voluntarily until the work was finished.

CHAPTER FIVE: SUMMARY OF NEW MEASURES

Fixed Penalty Notices

- We will consult the police to see whether FPNs are needed for other offences
- We will extend the FPN for disorder schemes enable other persons accredited by the Chief Constable to issue notices.
- We will enable Local Authorities and other accredited persons to issue FPNs for a wider range of offences related to environmental quality, such as fly-posting or graffiti.
- We will enable officers to issue notices to 16-17 year olds for disorder initially as a pilot exercise.

Injunctions

- We will promote the use of existing injunctions, which can be used by local authorities to tackle anti-social behaviour.

Anti-social Behaviour Orders (ASBOs)

- Better use of orders on conviction for anti-social behaviour by defining the role of the Crown Prosecution Service and other agencies.
- From April, county courts will be able to use their new powers under the Police Reform Act 2002 to make orders against defendants who are appearing in related proceedings. We will extend this power further so that when a tenant is being evicted, for example, due to the anti-social behaviour of a family member or friend the court can also make an order against the person responsible for the anti-social behaviour.
- Applicant agencies who have obtained orders have automatic access to breach prosecutions in the youth court to monitor the case and keep witnesses and victims informed.
- We will give local authorities new powers to enable them to prosecute breaches of ASBOs.

Community accountability

- We will lift automatic reporting restrictions on orders on conviction made in the youth court in order to ensure appropriate publicity of the details of the order.
- We will develop new proposals to pilot Community Justice Centres to deal with low-level disorder offences and anti-social behaviour including housing related matters.

Making fines more effective

Measures in the Courts Bill currently before Parliament will introduce:

- A discount for prompt payment in line with agreed terms, or increases if the defendant fails to pay on time, or fails to contact the court to reschedule payments.
- Fines officers to manage the collection and enforcement of outstanding financial penalties. This will include the ability to deduct fines from salaries or benefits.

Printed in the UK by The Stationery Office Limited
on behalf of the Controller of Her Majesty's Stationery Office
Id 133871 03/03 77240